The Solitary Self

Heretics

Series Editor: Mark Vernon

Heretics can be the most profound thinkers. They engage with a tradition of thought or received wisdom and, finding it wanting, seek not to dismiss it but to reform or reinterpret it. The books in this series seek to engage with various traditions in science, philosophy and religion in order to highlight where the authors believe something has gone wrong, and to explore the ways in which they believe things can be significantly improved.

The Solitary Self
Mary Midgley

Forthcoming

Against Humanism
Tim Crane

Credo
Mary Warnock

The Solitary Self

Darwin and the Selfish Gene

Mary Midgley

ACUMEN

First published in 2010 by Acumen
Reprinted 2010, 2011

Acumen Publishing Limited
4 Saddler Street
Durham
DH1 3NP
www.acumenpublishing.co.uk

ISBN: 978-1-84465-253-2

British Library Cataloguing-in-Publication Data
A catalogue record for this book is available from the British Library.

Typeset in Warnock Pro.
Printed by Ashford Colour Press Ltd, UK.

Contents

Introduction

On being social

The topic of this book is individualism. It starts from a discussion of Darwin because he is now widely credited – or blamed – as the source of the strange, drastic form of individualism that is current today. He did not actually invent that doctrine. In fact, his views about human relations were quite contrary to it. They centred on the natural, human affections and fears that bind us together, on the conflicts that arise among those natural feelings and on the ways in which we try to arbitrate these conflicts. More than many thinkers, Darwin fully recognized the crucial importance of conflict in our lives. And this makes his views much more realistic, and so more interesting, than the simple current dogmas of neo-Darwinism.

It seems worth while to get the record straight about this because Darwin's authority and influence, which are now considerable, should not be used to back views that are not his. Besides that, however, the whole topic is central to us now because individualism is giving us real difficulties today. Although it is a guiding ideal for our age, accepted as a main achievement of the Enlightenment, it takes many different forms. In a general way we take it to be the saving sense that people are distinct from one another and must all be considered separately. And in practical politics we often try to get them this kind of freedom. Yet the resulting isolation often makes for loneliness and loss of meaning. Moreover, campaigns for liberation become confused because different individuals have different aims. Free trade can produce very unfree conditions for workers – free house-building can produce cities horrible to live in – but there are individuals on all sides. And so forth.

Clashes like this constantly force us, in practice, to invoke other principles besides individualism in order to decide *which* individuals, and *which* factors in their lives, should have precedence. Different ideologies, favouring different kinds of freedom, make all the difference to what counts as individualism. The ideology that is most influential here at present is essentially a commercial one, centring on the importance of free competition – free enterprise – the deregulation of business. And the philosophic backing now given to it is the supposedly Darwinian belief in natural selection as a pervasive, irresistible cosmic force.

Neo-Darwinian theorists offer this force as the final explanation, not just of evolution, but of all sorts of deep social, physical and metaphysical mysteries as well. Thus it seems that competition lies at the heart of the universe. And what explains our own lives is the unbridled, savage competition between the genes that supposedly rule us. This is the vision that Richard Dawkins offers us in answer to questions about human destiny in his book *River Out of Eden*, which is boldly subtitled *A Darwinian View of Life*: "The universe we observe has precisely the properties we should expect if there is, at bottom, no design, no purpose, no evil and no good, nothing but blind pitiless indifference … DNA neither cares nor knows. DNA just is. And we dance to its music" (1995: 155).

Of course this is meant as a myth, not a detailed scientific thesis, and some people may therefore think it doesn't matter. But our imaginations feed on striking myths like this much more than we notice. After all, colourful documents such as *The Communist Manifesto* and *The Book of Revelations* have had much more influence than most philosophical writings. In this book I have concentrated on Dawkins's formulations of the neo-Darwinist worldview rather than on more moderate statements because their very extremeness makes them instructive. Their strong colours bring out the disturbing implications of ideas that pass as usable when they are expressed more vaguely. And these ideas, in their more discreet, muted forms, are still very widely shared today, even though they have been often attacked. Many people who would wince at Dawkins's rhetoric probably do not notice that they are taking much of his worldview for granted.

The notable thing about his story here is not its atheism but its fatalism. The drama that it presents of helpless humans enslaved by a callous fate-figure is, of course, not new and, like all such myths, it conveys not just meaninglessness but a positive, sinister meaning – the presence of an active oppressor. The new thing about the current version is merely the cast-list and the backing provided for the story. Fatalism is now offered, not as just one possible philosophical attitude among others with reasons given for and against it, but as a *fact* backed by the tremendous authority of science. The cosmic bully whom it invokes is now not a pagan deity but a chemical, DNA, a part of our own cells that – since we, like other organisms, are just lumbering robots ruled by it – is invoked as the true source of our acts. And the only motivation that it supplies for us is unqualified egoism: "selfishness".

This story combines two distinct kinds of reduction: the social atomism, which splits human society into separate, isolated individuals; and the physicalist reduction, which splits each individual into the units of his own body. These two strategies don't seem to be necessarily connected; indeed, they are hardly compatible. Blurring them together produces a highly confused ideology, but their common reductive quality makes people see them both as scientific. Taken together, they mean that all human action is unavoidably selfish. This message of an unavoidable doom is not cancelled by Dawkins's occasional claims that free choice is still possible, or that there might be some slight natural altruistic motivation, because these passages are so contrary to the rest of his argument that they are clearly only added as opium for the sensitive. The doctrine is meant to be a comprehensive one.

The varieties of egoism

That claim to comprehensiveness is, of course, not a new one. Thomas Hobbes (1588–1679) resoundingly launched the same claim that all action is self-interested three centuries ago. He did this as a challenge to feudalism: a protest against the aristocratic ethic of chivalry, which told people to lay down their lives in wars of religion. Hobbes wanted them to become selfish enough to stop doing this and form a consensual society, so he told them that they could easily do so because really they were totally selfish already. His very sensible bourgeois protest sowed the seed that grew into Enlightenment individualism, drawing attention to all sorts of ways in which individuals were actually being oppressed. But, as happens with such seminal ideas, the story was far too simple to stand much wear.

People quickly grasped that, selfish though we may all often be, it is absurd to say that we are all always ruled by self-interest. If we were, no such word as *selfish* could ever have been invented. Even apart from altruism, much of human action is either thoughtless or actually self-destructive. Besides this obvious fact, however, as wars declined and people started to attend more to their individual lives, the focus of thought gradually shifted from public to private matters – away from "interest" – outward profit or advantage – towards the quality of life itself. People began to concentrate less on prudence and more on autonomy, on authentic experience, on living your own life rather than simply following other people's example. And here their prophet was not Hobbes, or a pleasure-theorist such as Jeremy Bentham, but Nietzsche, whose many unreconciled insights on these matters still keep us busy today.

Thus, the whole problem of the meaning of self-interest and self-fulfilment – and indeed of what selves themselves actually are – has proved to be much more troublesome than it looked in Hobbes's day. Attempts to understand selves have long produced an uproar of controversy. Like Darwin, we today already know that our motivation is indeed complicated and is riven by conflicts. What we most want, therefore, is to see how best to deal with those conflicts. And we know that no simple, comprehensive theory of motivation is likely to be much use for this.

It is striking, then, that neo-Darwinians have ignored all these difficulties and have reintroduced egoism in its simplest, most comprehensive form as mere universal "selfishness". They do not take this, as Hobbes did, to centre on each individual's alarm about his own safety, making everybody keen to form a social contract. Instead, their whole emphasis is on competition itself as something permanent and incurable, a basic pattern in the cosmos. Their preferred imagery for it from human life is mostly commercial, military or criminal:

> Like successful Chicago gangsters, our genes have survived, in some cases for millions of years, in a highly competitive world. This entitles us to expect certain qualities in our genes. I shall argue that a predominant quality to be expected in our genes is ruthless selfishness. This general selfishness will usually give

rise to selfishness in individual behaviour [and any possible exceptions to this are negligible] ....

We are born selfish. (Dawkins 1976 [hereafter TSG]: 2–3)

If this conclusion were printed as an explicit theory of human motivation it would probably not look very impressive. The reason why it passes here as just one more metaphor, rather than as bad psychology, is that this discussion does not, officially, concern motives at all but is purely a biology lesson: an exposition of genes and the workings of natural selection. Readers are too cowed by the general aura of physical science – too impressed by the thought that they are being educated in the grand secrets of evolution – to complain about what is obviously poor thinking on general subjects.

Natural selection does not need drama

The science itself does not, however, actually support this myth. By now, plenty of biologists have pointed out that it is misleading to dramatize natural selection in this way. Competition is not, in fact, any more prevalent in the biosphere than cooperation. Indeed, it is inevitably less prevalent, because competition cannot get started until there has been a great deal of cooperation to build up the individual competitors. For instance, as we now know, the chloroplasts and other organelles within our cells were almost certainly once separate beings, distinct creatures that ended up playing their instruments in our internal orchestra because they had prospered inside cells. They found that a social life suited them, as, of course, it also suits us. And again, the kind of cooperation that exists between the microbes in our guts and the rest of our bodies, or between flowering plants and pollinators, is widespread.

Of course, prophets who are set on finding a competitive meaning can, if they like, insist that this is all just a wily pretence. But at this point their myth-making intention surely becomes obvious and must raise questions about their own motives. They are not reporting facts but imposing a particular interpretation on them, an interpretation that needs to be justified at its own level in the context of the rest of thought, not privileged as part of science. In fact their vision is not really science but a species of general thinking that uses scientific imagery to give force to its ideas. In this it is like the mechanistic thinking of the Newtonian age, dominated by the imagery of clockwork. That thinking has, of course, been useful in many ways, but its limited imagery has increasingly made it misleading, particularly in physics.

Besides this needless dramatization, however, biologists are now beginning to complain of something more central to neo-Darwinism. They are saying that the role of natural selection in evolution has itself been much exaggerated. This kind of competition cannot be the sole cause of new developments for a simple logical reason; namely, because no filter can be the sole cause of what flows out of it. Strainers strain out coffee grounds; they do not create coffee. Similarly, it is becoming clear that the complex items we see must have had internal causes as well as the filters that eliminated other forms. Some kind of self-organization – some set of positive tendencies within the substance of living things – is necessary to produce these new forms. Organisms must have been so framed as to shape themselves in one way rather than another. The resulting phenomena are so complex that trial and error alone could never have done this job, even if there had been infinite time to do it in.

Brian Goodwin points this out in considering the case of an ant colony where the ants all move in rhythm and rest harmoniously in concert:

It is clear that natural selection in no way explains the *origin* of the rhythmic activity-pattern in the brood-chamber ... It is an example of self-organization as the origin of a biological form. It is clear that any biological form must arise spontaneously before it can be selected, and one of the jobs of science is to explain how this might occur .... Darwinism and neo-Darwinism propose that new forms arise as a result of random change in genes. This may well be the case, but we are then left asking how the observed patterns and form of organisms are generated from known properties. What makes them possible? Complexity theory addresses the question of origins, providing an explanation by describing a pattern of interactions in a complex system from which the form can arise.

(1988: 40)

Thus, as Ilya Prigogine and Isabelle Stengers explained in *Order Out of Chaos* (1984), new patterns arise spontaneously, both in the inorganic and the organic world. Complex wholes such as an ant colony or a living body act *as wholes*. The structural properties that make this possible could not possibly be inferred from a knowledge of their separate parts. In fact, these ants do not act rhythmically in small numbers, but, when more of them are added, at a certain point they all do it at once.

One way and another, then, it emerges that, in general, the reductive thinking that theorizes about large-scale behaviour from analogy with the behaviour of small parts is not reliable or scientific. And in the case that now concerns us, where this interpretative method is used to expound Darwin's ideas, it is doubly misleading.

On psychological topics it totally distorts his message. It ignores the deeply social analysis that he actually gave of human behaviour, implying that he backed the crude, extreme individualism that is popular today. About the mechanism of evolution, on the other hand, the divergence from Darwin's views is less extreme but it is still serious. Darwin did indeed think that natural selection was very important and that it was probably the main cause of evolutionary change. But he said firmly that it could not be the only cause. He was sure there were other causes, even though he did not know what they were, and he thought they ought to be investigated. Thus the kind of enthusiasm that leads neo-Darwinists to inflate natural selection into a metaphysical principle pervading the universe was foreign to him and ought not to be sold under his name. Moreover, it distracts attention from what needs to be the next business of evolutionists, which is to understand the workings of self-organization.

***

This discussion obviously spreads over a panorama of topics. It has to do this simply because neo-Darwinism already jumbles together a mass of different arguments – metaphysical, biological, psychological and the rest – that need to be sorted out.

I think we owe its prophets a great debt for doing this. These topics really are connected and only the obsessive specialization of our age has made us neglect the relation between them. That relation, however, is a real one. It is entirely different from the connection that neo-Darwinism traces and is actually much more interesting.

When I thought of writing a book about this I saw that it would have to be either impossibly long or very short: just a sketch of the scene. From natural laziness I promptly chose the sketch, but this has made the book rather hard to summarize, since the different topics are connected in multiple ways and don't fall tidily into different sections. In fact, I have been circling around, or rather spiralling in on, what seems to me to be the central matter – which is how we conceive of our own individual nature – and in doing this I have often encountered the same topic repeatedly when it emerged in a different connection. With that apology, here is a rough summary of the book.

The first two chapters set out the general problem about the meaning of individualism and contrast what Darwin actually wrote on the importance of human sociability with neo-Darwinist separatist doctrines. Darwin emphasized how the development of human intelligence did not displace our species's highly complex range of social feelings but simply showed up conflicts among them and gradually suggested ways of dealing with these conflicts within society, notably morality. He explicitly rejected "selfishness" as an explanation of that morality. By contrast, Dawkins's book *The Selfish Gene*, as well as E. O. Wilson's *Sociobiology* and much other like-minded literature, use a very simple concept of selfishness derived not from Darwin but from a wider background tradition of Hobbesian social atomism, and give it as a general explanation of all behaviour, including that of humans. Chapter 2 discusses how this fits with the recent history of individualism, noting how, during the age of Ronald Reagan and Margaret Thatcher, various egoistic lines of thought converged to drive that doctrine ever further towards extremes. T. H. Huxley's earlier contribution to this pugnacious, egoistic interpretation of the struggle for existence is then noted, and the chapter ends by discussing controversies about group selection, in which the differences between Darwin's views and those of his supposed followers have been particularly striking.

In Chapters 3 and 4 the discussion turns to consider how Darwin's approach provides a useful change from the traditional philosophical debates in which Feeling and Reason have often been treated almost as opponents: separate, alternative faculties between which we are forced to choose. It explains Darwin's more usable model, in which rationality appears not as opposing feeling, but as the technique by which we bring our different kinds of feeling together. We see how helpful this perspective is for various problems and especially in making possible more realistic and constructive ideas of our relation to other animals. Darwin points out how much friendly order and cooperation – how much, indeed, of what we call humanity – there is already in the lives of other social animals and so undermines the notion that our own "animal nature" is something unmanageable and alien to us. His remark that much of the species difference is a difference "of degree and not of kind" is thus not really objectionably reductive. We note how, interestingly, Nietzsche, although he was a crucial prophet of Individualism, held views quite close to Darwin's on the evolution of morals.

The last two chapters round up a range of problems raised by the whole discussion so far and draw together the guiding threads that now emerge about them. These problems are, as I have suggested, of three main kinds: metaphysical, biological and psychological.

Metaphysical

First, led by the confident manifestos of the neo-Darwinists, we turn to the vast topic of cosmic meaning. Dawkins, Peter Atkins and others present the claim that the universe is meaningless as something factual, scientific and, more specifically, Darwinian. Their ground for considering the biosphere – or sometimes the whole cosmos – to be meaningless is that it is ruled by natural selection, which they present as simply a form of chance or, as Jacques Monod put it, a lottery. From this they conclude, as Steven Weinberg did at the end of *The First Three Minutes*, that "this is an overwhelmingly hostile universe ... The more the universe seems comprehensible, the more it also seems pointless" (1977: 154).

Darwin, however, made no such claim. Although he abandoned the rather naive Christianity of his childhood, he remained deeply impressed by cosmic order and still saw that order as akin to mind. Questions about the transcendent struck him not as meaningless, but as genuinely mysterious. He did not think we could expect certainty about them. And, of course, this view fits well with the thought that our faculties have largely been evolved for more modest uses.

But his tentative attitude also fits well with that of many physicists today who are struck by the coincidences that are emerging in the cosmic order: quite specific arrangements, such as those concerning the cosmological constant, for which no reason can be given. These are facts which seem highly improbable, but without which life, or indeed the whole material world, could never have existed. This leads a number of scientists – including some who are quite fiercely secular – to suspect that it may be more rational to conceive the universe as in some sense having a purpose or direction than to rule dogmatically that it must be random. Randomness is not, after all, something that could ever be scientifically established. Taking it for granted it is more a matter of temperament and intellectual fashion than of reasoning.

Biological

Scientists such as Brian Goodwin and Simon Conway Morris, along with philosophers such as Jerry Fodor, have developed this thought by noting that organisms too display active tendencies in their formation that are unmistakably independent of natural selection. Indeed, those tendencies are necessary to supply the raw material on which natural selection works. Mutations alone could not have produced all of it. Self-organization – natural creativity – which appears even at an inorganic level in such things as crystal formation, clearly accounts for many obvious features of organic form and seems likely to have played a part in more subtle ones as well. In the course of evolution, organisms have repeatedly converged towards certain forms for which no obvious mechanical reason emerges, but which seem to be naturally favoured. This suggests that selection from the outside is far less important in evolution than has often been suggested. And of course this selection itself is not actually very like a lottery, since the element of chance supplied by mutation is subordinate to the intelligible continuity provided by the environment. Lotteries are actually a highly artificial product of civilization, not something found in nature.

Thus, in the organic as well as the inorganic world, matter itself seems to contain tendencies to develop in one way rather than another. No extraneous, engineering God on the seventeenth-century model is needed to make this possible, although the traditional theological idea of an immanent God, pervading and animating the world, is perfectly compatible with it.

Darwin's own view on the matter is quite close to this conception. Although he did think that natural selection was the main cause of change in evolution, he was sure that it could not possibly be the sole cause. He never suggested it was a universal explanatory principle and he hoped that other evolutionary causes might later be investigated. And today's biologists are beginning to oblige him by doing this.

Psychological

In the last chapter, we come back to the crucial topic of human motives. Having seen that egoism cannot really be supported from outside by theories about evolution, we look at the two forms of it – the Hobbesian and the Nietzschean – that are still influential in our lives today and consider their various strengths and weaknesses in their own terms.

Both these ways of thinking have contributed a great deal to our current form of individualism and they each contain some precious, timeless insights. Neither of them, however, gives the universal guidance that people tend to expect from a moral prophet. Each of them was invented to guard against the excesses and abuses of a particular epoch. Hobbes stressed self-interest so as to debunk the exaltation of self-sacrifice that drove people into seventeenth-century wars of religion. His message, therefore, was: keep the peace and strengthen your society, because you personally want to be safe rather than gloriously dead. Nietzsche, however, arrived after that bourgeois lesson had been thoroughly learnt. He saw the need to reverse it, so he exalted solitude and self-assertion to debunk the complacent humbug of nineteenth-century life.

Both these protests have surely been necessary, both are still valuable. Both are elements in present-day individualism. But, as the conflicts between them show, each of them is only one part, not the whole, of the moral scene. We always have to decide afresh what is most needed in our own time.

1

Pseudo-Darwinism and social atomism

The mysterious roots of ethics

Amid all the celebrations in the year in which I write – the year of two great Darwinian anniversaries; the 150th of the publication of his great book, the 200th of his birth – it is rather striking that so little has been heard about Darwin's idea of morality. Indeed, people reading modern neo-Darwinist writings might well suppose that he took little interest in the matter or was unwilling to discuss it. Far from this, it was central to his understanding of human life, as he made clear at the start of the third chapter of *The Descent of Man*. There, after analysing the intellectual capacities of humans, he turned to consider their active tendencies and found there something even more important. He wrote:

> I fully subscribe to the judgment of those writers who maintain that *of all the differences between man and the lower animals, the moral sense or conscience is by far the most important.* This sense, as Mackintosh remarks, "has a rightful supremacy over every other principle of human action"; it is summed up in that short but imperious word *ought*, so full of high significance.

> It is the most noble of all the attributes of man, leading him without a moment's hesitation to risk his life for a fellow-creature; or after due deliberation, impelled simply by the deep feeling of right or duty, to sacrifice it in some great cause.
>
> (Darwin 1981: 70, first emphasis added)[1]

He pointed out the difficulty that philosophers have always found in understanding the source and meaning of this compulsion. Properly hesitant about approaching so vast a question, he explained what would be his own, quite limited, angle on it:

> This great question has been discussed by many writers of consummate ability; and my sole excuse for touching on it is the impossibility of here passing it over and because, as far as I know, *no-one has approached it from the point of view of natural history.* (*Ibid.*: 71, emphasis added)

This, indeed, he does. And the remarkable thing is that he avoids the usual kinds of reduction in doing it. He does not explain morality away by pretending that it is really something else. Nor does he "explain" it by reciting scientific facts that are not relevant to it. What he does is to *put it in context*: to show it as an intelligible reaction for social creatures who live, as we do, on an earth that constantly confronts them with difficulties and who have developed there in the kind of way that we have.

Understanding that natural context does, however, deeply affect the meaning of morality itself. It throws a new light on the relation between reason and feeling, something that has always been a stumbling block to moral philosophers. Unlike most modern evolutionary

---

1. All further quotations from Darwin are from this book, *The Descent of Man*, unless another one is named.

psychologists, who assume that we fully understand the institutions we have now and merely speculate about their evolutionary causes, Darwin grapples with real contemporary issues about our moral constitution. This means that he can paint a picture of our social nature that is both shrewd and original, a picture that fits better both with evolutionary considerations and with actual human behaviour than those we are most familiar with today.

The invention of Darwinism

There are two reasons why this important discussion has been neglected. One is the very narrow, stereotypic idea of Darwin's thought that has lately prevailed. During the last half-century, people have seen him primarily as the discoverer of natural selection: the engineer who managed to bolt that final piece of mechanism into the story of evolution, thus explaining, at last, how it can plausibly have taken place. Both supporters and opponents have concentrated on this, which is indeed central to his work. But he also took much more trouble than is usually noticed to work out the *meaning* of this change: to consider just how it should affect the rest of our thinking, especially the way we think about ourselves.

On this topic, very crude ideas were at once attributed to him in his own day by people, such as Herbert Spencer, who ought to have known better. Still more surprisingly, this process has continued busily in our own time, establishing the notion of a confused reductive ideology called Darwinism that is actually quite alien to his thought. Often this doctrine is simply taken to be a vindication of savage, unbridled competition. As Steven Rose says, "Darwinism was seen variously as justifying imperialism, racism, capitalism and patriarchy ... Today, journalists refer to board-room struggles and takeover battles for companies as 'Darwinian'" (1997: 175). And

James Le Fanu, who blames not just evolutionary theory but Darwin personally for nearly all today's distresses, writes:

> The uncritical endorsement of misleading explanations can have grievous consequences. We have glimpsed in an earlier chapter some of these in the propagation of eugenic policies and the absurdities of socio-biology. But there is more, for, paradoxically, despite 150 years of remorseless scientific progress, we are left with a surprisingly pessimistic view of humanity as the perpetrators of the terrible destructive wars of the past century and the destroyers of the planet that sustains us. (Le Fanu 2009: 250)

It is, of course, always tempting to look for a single cause for one's troubles, but this seems to be going a bit far. In this book I want to show how misleading such talk is, not just in order to put the record straight but – more centrally – to bring the discussion of our nature back from wasteful fantasies to the central psychological topics that are of real concern to us, just as they were to Darwin. This shift is badly needed today because the travesty called *Darwinism* is now seriously influential. (About that, Le Fanu is right). The impression that we *ought* to accept crudely egoistic ideas – even if we don't like them – because they have been proved to be scientific is now quite widespread.

Individualism and social atomism

Besides this twisted notion of Darwinism, another potent factor that has led to neglect of this topic is the general difficulty that an individualistic age has in understanding the function of morality at all. Today, people tend to see "explaining morality" chiefly as a matter of discovering how beings who are each totally isolated can ever be called on to consider one another, a task that naturally proves impossible. The doctrine behind this approach is a shadowy but powerful belief in individual solitude, which may be called "Social Atomism". It is a combination of the deep individualism of our time – something that will occupy us throughout this book – and a prejudice about method: a general idea that it is always more scientific to consider separate components than the larger wholes to which they belong. Indeed, it is often believed that those larger wholes are actually less real. ("There is no such thing as society.")

Put together, these ideas imply that the right way to understand life, including human life, is not to look for the dominant patterns in it but to break it up into units – ultimate constituents – and find laws governing their interactions. In principle, these constituent atoms would not need to be physical ones. In fact, in the past various efforts have been made to analyse *consciousness* into mental units. Thus Hume treated it as a series of separate impressions, and later Wilhelm Wundt, trying to analyse introspection, made a number of suggestions about possible ways of breaking it into atoms. But these enterprises proved decidedly hard, so it is no surprise that today the atomizing task is being handled in physical terms, which always suit it better.

Thus, in biology, it began to appear in the mid twentieth century that the entity truly in charge of life was the gene, which was somehow more real than the organism it belonged to. As Brian Goodwin remarked:

> A striking paradox which has emerged from Darwin's way of approaching biological questions is that organisms, which he took to be the prime examples of living nature, have faded away to the point where they no longer exist as fundamental and irreducible units of life ....

Modern biology has come to occupy an extreme position in the spectrum of the sciences, dominated by historical explanations in terms of the evolutionary adventures of genes. Physics, on the other hand, has developed explanations of different levels of reality, microcosmic and macrocosmic, in terms of theories appropriate to these levels …. It is the absence of any theory of organisms as distinctive entities in their own right, with a characteristic type of order and organization, that has resulted in their disappearance from the basic conceptual structure of modern biology. They have succumbed to the onslaught of an overwhelming molecular reductionism.

(Goodwin 1994: 1–2)

The parallel with physics is indeed important, since physicists have already had to face this problem of combining explanations that work at different levels. When they lost the seventeenth-century belief in ultimate explanation by solid, separate, billiard-ball-like atoms they gradually saw how to use the surviving parts of Newtonian physics within a wider, more flexible range of different thought patterns, each of which is helpful for its own range of problems. Being no longer bound by the crude kind of materialism that saw the physical world as made of tangible objects such as stones, they could use a much more sensitive approach to topics such as energy and, indeed, consciousness. As many people have pointed out, this change in the notion of matter calls for some rethinking of the term *materialism* itself.

Biologists, however, have not interested themselves in these problems. Instead, as Goodwin says, they have continued to look for traditional "building blocks" – an unsuitable term that is still far too commonly used – in a way that leads them to use reductions of various kinds, extending explanatory schemes far beyond their natural scope. That range of atomistic reductions will concern us again and again in this discussion.

Reductive strategies

Reduction is always an attempt to simplify the conceptual scene. Often it springs from an impression that simplicity and clarity are always what is needed to make an explanation more scientific. But, where thought patterns have to fit a complex subject matter, this naturally does not work. The drawbacks of this slimming-down approach appear in some remarks of Lewis Wolpert's about the status of social science. Wolpert writes:

> There is a question whether the social sciences are really science … The peculiarity of the social sciences is the complexity of the subject-matter. (Wolpert 1992: 124–5)

> In a sense, all science aspires to be like physics and all physics aspires to be like mathematics. In spite of recent successes, biology has a long way to go when measured against physics or chemistry. Biologists can still be full of hope … but what hope is there for sociology acquiring a physics-like lustre?
>
> (*Ibid.*: 121)

The sentence about "aspiring" comes from Schopenhauer's remark that "all the arts aspire to the condition of music". It exalts purity and abstraction. But, whatever may be said of music, this ambition clearly makes no sense for science. Physics is *not* trying to be like mathematics nor like anything else. It does its own work, which is looking for general truths about the actual material world. It does not operate – or want to operate – as mathematics does, only at the level of thought; it wants real physical facts. Similarly, the other sciences, and indeed the humanities, each do their own special job of investigating particular chosen aspects of the world, so they need to use different conceptual patterns that suit those aspects.

Biology, then, is not an amateur science, struggling in an endless effort to become physics. Like history or logic, it has its own special work, which is to investigate life. And life is a quite peculiar phenomenon about which physics has absolutely nothing to say. This is why, during the past century, biologists of a reductive turn of mind have tried to play down this embarrassing topic altogether. Not only do they avoid talking about the concept of life itself (the standard dictionary of biology has no entry under the heading "life"), but they also try their damnedest to reduce life's distinctive patterns to ones found in things that are lifeless. In fact, they still seem haunted by the wish to ground their thought safely in Newtonian physics: to show that explanation always really terminates in inert, lifeless atoms that alone can be scientifically approved and in theories describing their connections. Thus, in *The Blind Watchmaker* Dawkins explains what is distinctive about life as follows:

> What lies at the heart of every living thing is not a fire, not warm breath, not a "spark of life". It is information, words, instructions. If you want a metaphor, don't think of fires and sparks and breath. Think, instead, of a billion discrete, digital characters carved in tablets of crystal. If you want to understand life, don't think about vibrant, throbbing gels and oozes, think about information technology. ... It is this that I was hinting at in the previous chapter, when I referred to the queen ant as the central data bank. (1986: 112)

Similarly Atkins observes, "Inanimate things are innately simple. That is one more step along the path to the view that animate things, being innately inanimate, are innately simple too" (1987: 53). This style of talk is designed to conceal the spontaneous creativity that is actually central to the concept of life behind a screen of documentation, as if the calculations that describe it were the thing itself.

Of course, logical clarity of theory and the precision of mathematics are important here, as they are for every sort of enquiry. But science always oscillates between that clarity and another pole that is even more important – truth to the outside world. Anyone can become clearer by becoming more abstract, by ignoring certain ranges of facts. But when the whole world is there waiting to be understood it is oddly perverse to ignore facts just for the sake of looking pure and "acquiring a physics-like lustre". And the notion of a "hard" science as being always a more abstract one is rather odd considering the ferociously hard work involved in working out conceptual schemes for understanding complex subject matters.

These confused aspirations are surely remnants of seventeenth-century dualism, thought-patterns that were specially devised to show matter and spirit as separate kinds of substance. The concept of *life* was always a serious embarrassment for that enterprise because it unmistakably brings the two things together. For that reason, people who think the glory of science depends on its sticking close to the concept of inert matter avoid the topic of life and use various sorts of reduction to show that it is not really needed.

This ambition to simplify thought for the sake of purity is surely central to the reductive shift from organisms to genes that we are now considering. It avoids complexity by breaking organisms into smaller units, dropping the thought patterns that were useful for understanding them as wholes. Goodwin is one of a number of biologists, some of whom we shall discuss later, who are now pointing out that biologists need to go back to this more holistic kind of understanding because it was actually very useful. As he says, this would not mean dropping the advances that come from studying genes, any more than the shift from a geocentric to a wider, Copernican view of the universe involved losing the knowledge previously gained about the earth on its own. It would merely put that knowledge in a wider, more realistic context. It is interesting that, in the case of the universe, nobody now complains that the more holistic, Copernican approach is unscientific.

It seems worth while asking, too, why the atomistic approach in biology stops at gene level. If smaller units are always more informative than larger ones, we might expect that it would be more scientific still to start from the physical particles – the quarks, and so on – of which the genes are composed, instead of taking either genes or individual human beings to be appropriate units, as is now done. However, this choice of a particular level is not exceptional. Scientific enquirers always concentrate their thinking at a particular scale because it interests them, often for reasons that have nothing to do with science. In fact, *holism* and *atomism* are not warring alternatives. They are complementary aspects of all scientific enquiry. But something particularly odd surely does occur at the point where a physical unit such as the gene begins to be thought of as directly explanatory for social and psychological patterns.

Why we don't quite fit

Darwin's approach to psychological questions is quite different. He starts by mildly pointing out that *Homo sapiens* is actually a sociable species, so that individual humans can be understood only in the context of the group they belong to. Like other social animals, they are not shaped for heroic solitude but for profound cooperation with others, living interdependently in friendly association: an obvious fact that has somehow got rather lost from our recent thinking. The feelings that make all this sociability possible – our natural affections, angers, loves, fears and dependencies – are, he says, the irreplaceable springs of our action and are closely comparable with the motives that make sociability possible in other species, although of course they are not exactly the same.

24

The great thing that differentiates our position from theirs is, he says, simply that we have added high intelligence to that ancient repertory of feelings in a way that makes us critical about them. We have become aware of endless conflicts between motives that simply do not trouble them. A chimpanzee that has attacked a friend in a fit of temper does not apologize afterwards. The two will normally be reconciled later in the day, but the victim is usually the one who makes advances, asking to be taken back into favour. There is no sign of remorse, nor, of course, do the bystanders show disapproval. This is all very unlike the human situation. The struggle to resolve the inner conflicts that lead to these troubles is the scene of all our special human difficulties, and so of our special successes. And the development of moral thinking is a crucial tool in that struggle.

At the end of his thoughts on the matter Darwin considers the relation between his view and the older, egocentric Hobbesian tradition. He writes:

> Philosophers of the derivative school of morals formerly assumed that the foundation of morals lay in a form of Selfishness … [but] According to the view given above, the moral sense is fundamentally identical with the social instincts, and in the case of the lower animals it would be *absurd to speak of these instincts as having been developed from selfishness.*   (97–8; emphasis added)

It may be necessary today to explain *why* this would be absurd; namely, because these animals are simply not clever enough to do it. They are not capable of the elaborate planning that would be needed to show good behaviour as profitable in the long run. Enlightened self-interest really does require a big cerebral cortex. He goes on:

They have, however, certainly been developed for the good of
the community ....

Thus *the reproach of laying the foundation of the most noble
part of our nature in the base principle of selfishness is removed*;
unless indeed the satisfaction which every animal feels when
it follows its proper instincts, and the dissatisfaction which it
feels when prevented, be called selfish.

(98–9, emphasis added)

Darwin on group selection

This is, of course, a "group-selectionist" view. It assumes that competition can just as well arise between two communities as between
two individuals, leading more cohesive societies to prevail over
fractious ones. Peter Kropotkin developed this approach very interestingly in his book *Mutual Aid.* Neo-Darwinian evolutionists,
however, decided that group selection was impossible and, accordingly, long ignored Darwin's espousal of it.

But, as we shall see, this disbelief in group selection has been well
challenged and there is now no scientific reason to reject Darwin's
view of it. After summing it up, he states his remarkable conclusion that the development of real morality – the kind that has actually been influential in the world – is not a mysterious paradox, but
makes perfectly good biological sense:

> The social instincts – *the prime principle of man's moral
> constitution* – with the aid of active intellectual powers and
> the effects of habit, naturally lead to the golden rule, "As ye
> would that men should do to you, do ye to them likewise"; and
> this lies at the foundation of morality.

(106, emphasis added)

This striking pronouncement is not, of course, just a pious hope, but a straightforward piece of ethology: a factual comment on the life pattern of a particular species. Naturally, Darwin is not suggesting that we always, or even often, obey the golden rule, or even interpret it sensibly. He is extremely careful to point out that we don't:

> It cannot be maintained that the social instincts are ordinarily stronger in man ... than the instincts of self-preservation, hunger, lust, vengeance etc. *Why then does man regret*, even though he may endeavour to banish such regret, that he has followed the one natural impulse rather than the other? And why does he further feel that he ought to regret his conduct? ... Man in this respect differs profoundly from the lower animals. (89, emphasis added)

But he is saying that the social elements in our constitution still unavoidably urge us in that direction despite our other wishes, producing chronic friction. In fact, he is noting *the unavoidable centrality of inner conflict in human life* and the need that this imposes for some kind of morality to resolve it. Less intelligent animals (he says) probably don't notice the clashes and so are not troubled by the need for resolution. But if their intelligence grew they too would become aware of inner discord, would note the anomalies and would have to respond more or less as we do, although the systems they would arrive at might be very different. Accordingly, he suspects that: "Any animal whatever, endowed with well-marked social instincts, would inevitably acquire a moral sense or conscience as soon as its intellectual powers had become as well-developed, or nearly as well-developed as in man" (71–2). In short, what makes our moral constitution possible – and indeed what makes us characteristically human – is *not* primarily our intellect.

27

It is the difficulty of combining that intellect with a given set of pre-existing social feelings.

Which kind of self?

This account of the role of morality in our life is surely more realistic than approaches that treat it as something external to our true nature – a set of alien rules imposed by parents or gods or rulers or by an abstract force called Reason or Society. What makes our conflicts so hard is that they are genuinely internal. Darwin surely shows here a sense of the real problems that infest human life, a sense that contrasts sharply with the simple accounts of motivation that some of his alleged followers now give. Thus Dawkins finds this topic quite straightforward:

> Be warned that if you wish, as I do, to build a society in which individuals co-operate generously and unselfishly towards a common good, you can expect little help from biological nature. Let us try to *teach* generosity and altruism because *we are born selfish*.　　　　(TSG 3, second emphasis added)

We should note that the word *selfish* here cannot have the special, technical meaning of "self-reproducing" that it is supposed to bear in Dawkins's discussions of "selfish genes". It cannot because in this passage it is explicitly applied to human motives, so it must have its everyday sense as the name of a single ruling motive, one that dominates all others. Dawkins sees that this dominance may make his readers doubt whether that motive can be reformed as he proposes, so at the end of the book he explains how we can improve it. Dismissing as implausible the idea that natural outgoing motives might contribute to this, he writes:

> Even if we look on the dark side and assume that individual man is fundamentally selfish, ... our conscious foresight ... could save us from the worst selfish excesses of the blind regulators ... We can see the long-term benefits of participating in a "conspiracy of doves", and we can sit down together to discuss ways of making the conspiracy work.   (TSG 215)

All we shall need, in short, is a little enlightened self-interest.

Rather surprisingly, Dawkins seems to propose this as quite a new suggestion, a remedy, so far untried, that will clear up the problem. Actually, of course, it is a very old idea, and is in fact the solution proposed by Hobbes, whose thoughts on the topic we shall look at presently. Dawkins, however, is clearly not confident that this will be enough, for he goes on:

> We can even discuss ways of deliberately cultivating and nurturing pure, disinterested altruism – *something that has no place in nature, something that has never existed before in the whole history of the world.* We are built as gene machines and cultured as meme-machines, but we have the power to turn against our creators. We, alone on earth, can rebel against the tyranny of the selfish replicators.
>
> (TSG 215, emphasis added)

Thus we find, to our great surprise, that – even though, as he has insisted for most of the book, "we" are merely lumbering robots, passive tools in the hands of the genes – this same "we" can yet (with a single bound) now become free to act, in effect, as supernatural beings, able to ignore the physical causes that have shaped us. The belief in the omnipotence of local physical causation that has been foundational during nine-tenths of the book suddenly dissolves at this point to allow free will and a happy ending.

Friendliness is natural

Why should such a drastic metaphysical miracle – something that "has no place in nature, something that has never existed before in the whole history of the world" – suddenly become necessary? This emergency only arises because the author accepts such a strangely simple and extreme account of human motivation. By treating the model of individual competition as a universal explanation for all social interactions, he, like others who claim to interpret Darwin today, makes spontaneous, uncalculating sociability look impossible. Darwin's own very different views on this matter are indigestible to those who claim to be his champions, which is no doubt why they have been ignored.

On the other hand a different public – one remote from that Dawkinsist tradition, one that is seriously interested in discussing moral issues – may well not even look at Darwin's views about them because they don't expect any enlightenment from him. And even if they do look at them they may be put off by his strong emphasis on our continuity with other social animals. Our tradition has so often relied on using crude, fantasy-laden stories about these other species – an imagery packed with villainous snakes, rats, wolves, hyenas and the rest – in order to establish its own moral status that Darwin's quiet acceptance of kinship still causes much disquiet. In fact, it is remarkable how he manages to balance a clear sense of the social capacities that make these creatures genuinely akin to us with an equal emphasis on the transformative effects of human intelligence, which make our lives so profoundly different. He makes it plain that parental affection guided by intelligence is a very different thing from parental affection without it.

Yet human parental affection still *is* parental affection: something bred into us because we have the good fortune to be mammals. Anyone who watches the parenting of cats, monkeys or indeed birds must see that their attitude is, in a deep sense, akin to ours. Similarly, young animals at play show affectionate regard for each other in the same way that young children do. These are obvious examples of the way in which humans are naturally linked to those around them by feelings of fellowship, just as other social creatures are. No monstrous metaphysical change is needed to explain the presence of spontaneous generosity.

Altruism, the direct wish to help others, is not a wild fantasy, not something that needs a conspiracy theory to account for it, but an everyday aspect of human motives. As Hume pointed out, a sympathetic involvement in what goes on around us is not optional; it is a basic part of our nature. We directly mind about these things: "The interests of society are not even on their own account indifferent to us; everything which contributes to the happiness of society recommends itself to our approbation and good-will ... the very aspect of happiness pleases us" (Hume 1894: 178–9)

Of course, this does not mean that we rejoice at everyone's happiness; the pleasure of those we dislike may positively annoy us. But for it to do so we do have to feel some concern about their feelings, however slight, and where we have no particular prejudice that concern does indeed naturally tend to be sympathetic. This obvious fact about empathy was, of course, ignored on principle during the Behaviourist epoch because it was deemed to be impossible.

Very interestingly, however, it has lately crept back into general acceptance owing to the discovery of mirror neurons. Now that neurologists can observe the brains of people and animals who are watching some transaction, they find that those brains do indeed echo in some degree the brain movements of those directly involved. This has allowed members of the scientifically minded public at last to accept as fact something that has certainly been a central element in their experience throughout their lives. They can now admit that we actually do perceive the anger, scorn, affection or suffering of those around us quite as directly as we see lights or hear noises, a feat that, however surprising, is an essential part of our equipment as social animals. Is it not interesting that the twentieth century could not admit this well-known fact until it was revealed through a machine?

Of course, outgoing motives based on this kind of empathy are patchy and unreliable. All kinds of other considerations can override them and that is why conscience is needed to support them. But spontaneously helpful acts are often seen, among other social species, from meerkats to elephants, and even more often among humans because humans are – as Darwin emphasized – by nature exceptionally sociable creatures. Of course, these acts do not always involve real sacrifice, but they quite often do. For instance, news items regularly report that when a human – or even some other animal – has been in danger of drowning, not only relatives but unconnected bystanders have spontaneously plunged in to the rescue, and can sometimes die in the attempt.

Is there something fishy about calling this kind of response *disinterested*? It certainly is not a scheme planned for one's own future profit, which is what "interested" actually means. It is indeed done to fulfil or satisfy one's own impulse, but that is true of all our actions, including completely self-destructive ones, so the point seems trivial. Bishop Butler put this neatly:

> To those who are shocked to hear virtue spoken of as disinterested, it may be allowed that it is indeed absurd to speak thus of it unless hatred, several particular instances of vice and all the common affections and aversions of mankind are acknowledged to be disinterested too.   (Butler 1969: 175)

Thus, a worker who rashly insults his boss has certainly not done it to promote his own interest; he has preferred to gratify his anger.

Similarly, someone who gives money that he can ill spare to a friend in trouble has done what he wanted but not what profited him. This is also true of suicides, and indeed of anyone who consciously puts their life in danger. All these kinds of action are quite ordinary. In fact, disinterested behaviour is really not unusual at all.

2
The background: egoism from Hobbes to R. D. Laing

Selves standing up for themselves

Since this is common knowledge, we may well ask why the sweeping claim to the dominance of selfishness was ever made. More broadly, why do so many people today (not only Dawkins) feel that they ought somehow to reduce all human motivation to self-interest? Why do they think it is realistic to give an account that conflicts with so much of the evidence?

This reductive project is, as I have suggested, part of the individualistic tradition that has been so important to us politically since Thomas Hobbes (whom we shall later consider) set it off that it sometimes seems to dominate our whole value system. Enlightenment thought in the West has been constantly engaged in separating individuals out from their surroundings: in securing that they have independent status, rather than being seen as merely parts of their families or nations. Independence and Originality, which are aspects of Freedom, are among the qualities that we most honour today. Indeed, freedom of one sort or another has gradually become a central ideal.

There are, however, many different things that we want to be free from. Campaigns in defence of freedom often start by attacking obviously indefensible forms of abuse and oppression. But, as the troublesome bonds are successively loosened, that process gradually leads us towards the idea that, ideally, each of us ought to stand altogether alone. At a political level, this notion dictates simple slogans such as "one man one vote" (or even, as awkward reformers eventually pointed out, "one person one vote"). But life is not all politics, and, as time has gone on, conflicts between different ideals – notably conflicts between various forms of freedom itself – have arisen to complicate the scene.

All commitments are restraints, yet we sometimes need commitment so as to be free to pursue our main projects. Again, free trade is now a prominent theme: in some contexts "a liberal" simply means one who supports free trade. But removing restraints on trade can mean oppression or slavery for those producing the goods traded. As people look more closely at these issues, clashes like this keep coming up, painting the scene in a wide variety of colours rather than simply in black and white.

The search for solitude

Black and white, however, have remained the favoured colours for discussions of individualism. It has repeatedly been treated as a single cause to be attacked or defended, and there have been interesting oscillations in its fortunes over time. For instance, during the Second World War and for some time after it, there was a strong surge of communal loyalty in Britain, leading to the foundation of the welfare state. Individualism was then less popular. Eventually, however, exhaustion and disillusion weakened that sentiment, so that many people were pleased when, in the 1970s, Margaret Thatcher raised the standard of competitive individualism.

This was also the time when a rather different type of individualism, romantic and rebellious rather than competitive and derived essentially from Nietzsche, seized the imagination of the young. During the 1960s, the idea that society, simply as such, was every individual's enemy – an outside force driving helpless people in alien directions – gained popularity and inspired a huge variety of movements, some of them directed against particular real evils of the time, some much more indiscriminate. The charismatic psychologist R. D. Laing, one of the sharpest prophets of this vision, expressed its insights in strong images that built up a new and intense individualist mythology. As Laing put it:

> From the moment of birth, when the stone-age baby first confronts its twentieth-century mother, the baby is subjected to these forces of outrageous violence, called love. ... The initial act of brutality against the average child is the mother's first kiss ... These forces are mainly concerned with destroying most of the baby's potentialities ... By the time the new human being is fifteen or so, we are left with a being like ourselves, a half-crazed creature, more or less adjusted to a mad world ....
>
> My theme is that we are effectively destroying ourselves by violence masquerading as love.   (Clay 1996: 100–101)

In the early 1960s, when I first taught in universities, Laing's writings, along with those of Sartre and Marcuse, were the students' bibles. What did Laing actually teach them? Primarily, of course, to escape from their parents, but what after that? When challenged, he always said that he was not against love itself, nor against families. Officially, his chief concern was positive – to get a more honest expression of feelings within the family – and he also wanted to protest against larger evils such as the nuclear arms race. But his hugely sweeping rhetoric naturally suggested simply that everybody should be left alone. Individuals must shun all outside influence. They needed only to "do their own thing".

Of course, the problem he faced here is real. How can bad traditions ever be broken if children are constantly influenced by their parents? He evidently hoped, like Plato, that children could be insulated from those traditions provided that their parents did not get too close to them. But unfortunately close attachment is necessary if people are to grow into social beings at all. That stone-age baby does not arrive already provided with a stone-age worldview, even if such a worldview were actually what was needed. To grow at all it must take in whatever kind of mental food is on offer around it. However faulty that diet may be, any improvements will have to come later.

Laing, however, will not have this. His diagnosis is in fact strikingly like Rousseau's, even though his prescription is quite different. On the first page of his *Emile*, Rousseau wrote:

> Tender, anxious mother, I appeal to you. You can remove this young tree from the highway and shield it from the crushing force of social conventions ... From the outset *raise a wall round your child's soul*; another may sketch the plan; you alone should carry it into execution. (Emphasis added)

This suggests that the mother can stay inside the wall. Of course, it soon turns out that the tutor will take her place there, but evidently Rousseau did still think that somebody must train that tree, that new ideas to replace old social conventions must be provided. Laing, by contrast, tolerates no suggestions about input at all. His message seems to be entirely negative. Non-directive therapists such as Carl Rogers similarly ruled – although less brutally – that each person's salvation lay only in self-actualization. Outsiders, particularly therapists, should avoid making any suggestions that might distort this.

Economists too, of course, still defined rationality wholly in terms of self-interest. They had long been doing this, but they now had an unaccustomed chorus to support them in it. Economists were also largely responsible for launching the model of game theory, a concept that, with its simple competitive structure, quickly became standard issue for any social theories that aspired to be up to date and scientific. All these prophets combined to give a new personal force and immediacy to egoistic doctrines that had previously been seen as more abstract and political. And when *The Selfish Gene* was published, in 1976, it was at once taken as both a confirmation and development of this self-actualizing spirit.

Thus, for a good forty years this striking solipsistic propaganda became the orthodoxy of the age. It was, of course, sometimes challenged. For instance, as early as 1964 Eric Berne published *Games People Play: The Psychology of Human Relationships*, calling for cooperative interdependence. As Berne put it, "if you are not stroked, your spinal cord will wither". But for a long time the zeitgeist brushed all such suggestions aside. Only quite lately has the financial crash, which was so clearly the result of systematic, conscientious selfishness, begun to crack open public certainty about this gospel. This interruption probably accounts for the recent widespread interest in discussions of "the social brain": that is, of natural human cooperativeness and mutual suggestibility. Madeleine Bunting, a *Guardian* journalist, explains how astonishing she finds these proposals. Can it really be true, she asks, that:

> put crudely, we are social creatures with an inbuilt tendency to co-operate and seek out each other's approval, and that this is probably more important in determining our day-to-day behaviour than narrowly conceived self-interest. ... This is the kind of stuff which challenges almost everything you're used to thinking about yourself. (Bunting 2009: 27)

That these ideas, which, at any other epoch, would have seemed as obvious to everybody else as they did to Darwin, can now strike educated people as startling discoveries is a remarkable tribute to the power of cultural habit. Aristotle, for instance, certainly thought he was merely stating something boringly obvious when he remarked that "no-one would choose the whole world on condition of being alone, since man is a political/social animal whose nature it is to live with others" (*Politics* 1.2, 1252b). But there is no truth so obvious that it cannot sometimes be concealed by a shift of moral and intellectual fashion.

The Selfish Gene was not, of course, intended as a political or social statement. But, at the time when it came out, Dawkins's emphatic use of the word *selfish* was both an expression of the zeitgeist and a stimulus to its further development. The choice of the word "selfish" is actually quite a strange one. This word is not really a suitable one for what Dawkins wanted to say about genetics because genes do not act alone. As he himself points out in *The Selfish Gene*, "it is not easy, indeed it may not even be meaningful, to decide where one gene ends and the next one begins" (TSG 23). He himself later remarked that "co-operative gene" would have been a better description, and he emphasized the point in celebrations of the book's twenty-fifth anniversary. But, on the topic of human motivation, it was then just what people wanted to hear.

It is interesting that Bishop Butler, writing in the early eighteenth century, reports a similar vogue for defending selfishness in his own day, a vogue that was probably a long-term reaction against the seventeenth-century religious wars. After remarking that we do, of course, naturally tend to favour our own interests, Butler writes:

> There is also I know not what of fashion on this side; and, by some means or other, the whole world almost is run into the extremes of insensibility towards the distresses of their fellow-

creatures; so that general rules and exhortations must always
be on the other side.   (Butler 1969: 103)

The egoist philosopher whom he cites as central to this vogue is
Hobbes, whose diatribes against useless self-sacrifice did indeed
have a huge influence. Indeed, Hobbes may be regarded as the
inventor of the modern supposedly independent self. Writing in a
cold fury against the kind of feudal morality that had been used to
justify those wars, Hobbes expressed the claims of the beleaguered
self in deathless prose that has continued to echo through the works
of his followers (including many who have never read him), and still
does so today.

Enter the gladiators: Thomas Huxley at war with the cosmos

Deathless prose, however, does tend to oversimplify things. In our
tradition, this egoist doctrine has been promoted in areas of life
that Hobbes himself never professed to deal with. But in this book
we are primarily interested in understanding the tradition itself and
its lasting influence on our lives. Our topic is Hobbism, a doctrine
that was always extreme and has naturally been conveyed through a
salvo of striking phrases, so I shall not try here to examine Hobbes's
own more subtle and various meanings. Instead, what concerns us
is the influence of this kind of thinking, Thus, for instance, T. H.
Huxley, clearly an ardent Hobbist, confidently describes the lifestyle
of primitive humans like this:

> The weakest went to the wall, while the toughest and shrewdest,
> those best fitted to cope with their circumstances, but not the
> best in another way, survived. Life was a continuous free fight,
> and beyond the limited and temporary relations of the family,

41

the Hobbesian war of each against all was the normal state of
existence.   (Huxley 1888: 165)

Since Huxley's day, however, we have learnt much more about the
lives of hunter-gatherers and about those of our primate relatives.
There is now a mass of new evidence that shows up his exciting story
as pure mythology. Nor is his better-known description of animal
life any more realistic. He writes:

> From the point of view of the moralist, the animal world is
> on about the same level as a gladiators' show. The creatures
> are fairly well treated, and set to fight; whereby the strongest,
> the swiftest; and the cunningest live to fight another day. The
> spectator has no need to turn his thumb down, as no quarter
> is given.   (*Ibid.*)

Here again, since his time observation has shown that this is simply
a mistake. Actual fighting plays a very limited part in the lives of
animals. Indeed it should have been obvious that the highly artificial lives of gladiators – slaves kept exclusively for show-fighting –
could not possibly be a model for those of any wild creature. Nobody
finances animals; they have their own living to make.

The gap between Huxley's and Darwin's views here is the gap
between a fantasy – a communal fantasy that has been very strong
in our tradition – and direct observation. It starts from their quite
different backgrounds. Darwin, a country boy living close to animals
all his life, very early learnt to understand their forms of communication. He viewed them as intelligible fellow creatures, beings akin
to him whose attitudes he could often grasp. He was very interested
in the different behavioural languages that different species use for
this communication, and in his excellent book *The Expression of the
Emotions in Man and Animals* (1872) he traced out how various

positions, various movements and muscles, were suitably adapted to express their owners' different moods.

In all the recent Darwinolatry, this important book too has been strangely neglected. The reason for its neglect is that Darwin's relatively sympathetic, realistic attitude to other species went right out of fashion when the behaviourists insisted that their mechanistic, depersonalized approach was the only scientific way to study mental life. Eventually, ethologists such as Konrad Lorenz and Niko Tinbergen resisted this by suggesting that we can actually learn more by using the powers of social perception that evolution has given us – as Darwin used them – than by switching those powers off and pretending that the creatures around us are made of clockwork. Since their time, a flood of careful accounts by people, such as Jane Goodall, who have taken the trouble to observe the natural life of animals systematically, has shown how far the facts here diverge from the fantasies of the earlier tradition. Thus, gradually, Darwin's direct approach is becoming accessible again today, even though many scientists – unlike him – still find it embarrassing to admit that they can understand what their dogs and cats have been telling them for years.

Trouble with the brutes

Huxley's upbringing was quite different. Like most modern urban scholars, he lacked this vital background of experience. A town boy from a rather poor family, he was passionately curious about all natural phenomena, but his spontaneous interest centred on structure rather than on social detail. He would have liked to become an engineer, but since no such opportunity offered he gladly became a biologist and then naturally concentrated on problems of anatomy. He was wholly convinced by Darwin's account of how life had developed and he eagerly pressed the public to accept it. Yet he was distressed by the difficulty of asking people to accept that they were descended from animals:

> It would be unworthy cowardice were I to ignore the repugnance with which the majority of readers are likely to meet [these conclusions] ... No-one is more strongly convinced than I am of the vastness of the gulf between civilized man and the brutes, or is more certain that, whether *from* them or not, he is assuredly not *of* them.   (Huxley 1886: 234)

The only way (he says) in which we can make ourselves accept this odious possibility is by taking pride in our success at becoming totally unlike our ancestors:

> Thoughtful men, once escaped from the blinding influences of traditional prejudice, will find in the lowly stock from which man has sprung the best evidence of the splendour of his capacities, and will discern in his long progress through the Past a reasonable ground of faith in his attainment of a nobler Future.   (*Ibid.*)

Huxley's disgust at these thoughts stemmed mainly from the old tradition of seeing animals simply as embodied vices. But it partly came, too, from the melodramatic imagery by which (as we have seen) he conceived of natural selection wholly in terms of warfare and gladiatorial games. This destructiveness seemed to him to be central to the workings of evolution and, indeed, to the workings of the whole universe. He insisted, therefore, that evolution, far from being a reliable guide to morals as Herbert Spencer had suggested, was, along with the whole "cosmic process" behind it, a hostile, anti-human force that must at all costs be resisted:

Ethical nature, while born of cosmic nature, is necessarily at enmity with its parent.   (Huxley 1893: viii)

The ethical process is in opposition to the principle of the cosmic process, and tends to the suppression of the qualities best fitted for success in that struggle. ... [Man must therefore be] perpetually on guard against the cosmic forces, whose ends are not his ends.   (*Ibid.*: 44)

Laws and moral precepts are directed to the end of curbing the cosmic process.   (*Ibid.*: 82, emphasis added)

But what sort of power can you use if you want to overcome the cosmic process? From what stronghold outside the cosmos can you launch this strange campaign? And where does the motivation for that Oedipal struggle come from? Like Dawkins, Huxley has to posit a metaphysical miracle here in order to account for human moral sensibilities, simply because he has ignored their real source. Being blind to the rich variety of natural motives among animals, he takes it that our "animal nature" cannot possibly be the source of anything good. He certainly cannot conceive of what Darwin called the social instincts – the more benign side of human nature – as making moral development possible.

Struggles and melodramas

About natural selection, Huxley's mistake, in which plenty of people have followed him, is to treat what are really metaphorical terms such as the *struggle for existence* literally, as meaning actual fighting. Darwin himself pointed out this error in the third chapter of *The Origin of Species*, when he wrote:

I should premise that I use the term Struggle for Existence in a large and metaphorical sense, *including dependence of one being on another*, and including (which is more important) not only the life of the individual but success in leaving progeny .... A plant on the edge of a desert is said to struggle for life against the drought, though more properly it should be said to be dependent on the moisture .... When we reach the Arctic regions, or snow-capped mountains, or absolute deserts, the struggle for life is almost exclusively with the elements.

(Darwin 1985: 116, 121–2, emphasis added)

In fact, the military metaphor, which we still use so often, systematically misleads us. "Struggle" can mean simply any kind of difficulty or effort. It can indeed include fighting, but it can equally include cooperation in face of natural stresses.

Theorists, however, have been so strongly attracted by the pugnacious interpretation that they have treated it as a central part of Darwinism. As Kropotkin noted:

It happened with Darwin's theory as it always happens with theories having any bearing upon human relations. Instead of widening it according to his own hints, his followers narrowed it still more .... They came to conceive the animal world as a world of perpetual struggle among half-starved individuals thirsting for each other's blood. They made modern literature resound with the war cry of woe to the vanquished, as if it were the last word in modern biology. They raised the "pitiless" struggle for personal advantages to the height of a biological principle which man must submit to as well ....

But Huxley's view of nature had as little claim to be taken as a scientific deduction as the opposite view of Rousseau, who

saw nothing in nature but love, peace and harmony destroyed
by the accession of man.   (Kropotkin 2006: 22)

That is the spirit in which Dawkins, who is really a Huxleyan
rather than a Darwinian thinker, declares that "Tennyson's famous
phrase … 'nature red in tooth and claw' sums up our modern
understanding of natural selection admirably" (TSG 2). His readers
are likely to suppose that this refers to literal fighting, or preda-
tion, or at least internecine competition. In fact, the main theme of
his book is a metaphorical account of competition between *genes*,
entities that do not bleed and produce no redness. Tennyson, of
course, was talking about extinctions of species, which do not bleed
either and often succumb to something as undramatic as lowered
temperature.

In ordinary animal life, by contrast, there is, of course, a great
deal of death and a great deal of bleeding, but increased knowledge
has shown that competition is not the main cause of it. As Arthur
Peacocke remarks:

> It has taken modern biologists to restore the balance in our
> view of the organic world by reminding us that, as Simpson
> said, "To generalise … that natural selection is overall and
> even in a figurative sense the outcome of struggle, is quite
> unjustified under the modern understanding of the process
> … Struggle is sometimes involved, but it usually is not …
> Advantage in differential reproduction is usually a peaceful
> process in which the concept of struggle is really irrelevant".
>   (1986: 54–5)

Thus, much of the immense sum of suffering and death in the animal
world, which so distresses us, does not come from fighting or active
competition but merely from adverse circumstances: background

conditions of climate and terrain. In fact, the reason why the world is so full of death is simply that it is full of life. There are always an immense number of creatures determined to live somehow, even in the hardest conditions, each of which must eventually die. They do indeed often get eaten, but this tends to give them a quick death, which is often better than a slow one.

Could all this death have been avoided? If single-celled creatures, reproducing by division, had been content to remain the only life forms, no predators could have developed and most individuals could have been – in some sense – immortal. What has favoured the short, difficult, separate lives that we now see, with their attendant tragedies, has been life's constant ambitious tendency to hang on and develop something new, however hard that may be. Kropotkin remarked that this is what attentive observers see in the wild:

> Two aspects of animal life impressed me most during the journey that I made in my youth in Eastern Siberia and Northern Manchuria. One was the extreme severity of the struggle for existence which most species of animals have to carry on against an inclement Nature .... The other was, that even in those few spots where animal life teemed in abundance, I failed to find – although I was eagerly looking for it – that bitter struggle for the means of existence, *among animals belonging to the same species*, which was considered by most Darwinists (though not always by Darwin himself) as the dominant characteristic of the struggle for life, and the main factor in evolution. [Instead] I saw Mutual Aid and Mutual Support carried on to an extent which made me suspect in it a feature of the greatest importance for the maintenance of life, the preservation of each species, and its further evolution.
>
> (Kropotkin 2006: xi)

As he points out, Darwin, an experienced observer of nature, understood this and therefore emphasized – especially in his later work – how, among social species, "the fittest" are not necessarily the strongest, nor indeed the cleverest, but the most sociable: those whose temperament most inclines them to friendly cooperation. That is indeed the message of *The Descent of Man* on these topics. And it is certainly why, during all the recent reverential noise about Darwin, so little attention has been paid to these discussions. They simply do not fit with the solipsistic tendencies of our age.

Doubts about group selection

This topic has had quite an interesting history. At first, biologists readily accepted Darwin's idea that mutual aid between individuals could well lead to cooperative groups surviving better than uncooperative ones. In the mid twentieth century, however, evolutionists decided that group selection could never prevail over individual selection within groups. George C. Williams and Dawkins ruled that competition between individuals was the only mechanism that could ever produce selection. This was treated as proven fact, although it seems actually to have been more of an ideological principal. Thus, as David Sloan Wilson puts it, the Age of Naïve Groupism was followed by a somewhat fervent Age of Individualism, in the spirit of which Williams ended his book *Adaptation and Natural Selection* with the exciting phrase, "I believe it is the light and the way" (1966: 124). Clearly this was fighting stuff, and in *The Extended Phenotype* Dawkins tells the story in equally dramatic terms, even claiming (against the evidence) that Darwin himself had shared this view: "We painfully struggled back, harassed by sniping from a Jesuitically sophisticated and dedicated neo-group-selectionist rearguard, until we finally regained Darwin's ground, the position that I am characterizing by the label 'the selfish organism'" (Dawkins 1982: 6). For Dawkins and his fellow sociobiologists this was, of course, only a stage on the way to claiming that the thing actually being selected was genes, which were therefore peculiarly real and in charge of the whole operation. Thus E. O. Wilson: "Beliefs are really enabling mechanisms for survival .... Thus does ideology bow to its hidden masters, the genes, and the highest impulses seem on closer examination to be metamorphosed into biological activity" (1978: 3–4).

Dawkins developed this thought in *The Selfish Gene* using a lush crop of imagery that represented them irresistibly as conscious agents and organisms as merely their passive vehicles. "The gene leaps from body to body down the generations, manipulating body after body in its own way and for its own ends ... before they sink into senility and death. The genes are the immortals" (TSG 36). All this flows from a rather strange way of thinking into which simple-minded materialists often slip, of treating microphenomena as if they were a separate cause of the large-scale activities they are involved in, rather than just one aspect of them. Thus, as Socrates pointed out in the *Phaedo*, someone who is asked why he is sitting here may answer by giving a detailed account of how his knees, hips and ankles work. But this kind of reply tends to leave the questioner feeling that his question has not been answered.

It is interesting to see how Dawkins avoids this kind of disappointment by suddenly revving up the gene drama to overwhelm it:

> [Genes] swarm in huge colonies, safe inside gigantic lumbering robots, sealed off from the outside world, communicating with it by tortuous indirect routes, manipulating it by remote control. They are in you and me; they created us, body and mind; and their preservation is the ultimate rationale for our existence. (TSG 21)

This story, however, depends entirely on its colouring, on the myth attached to it. With different imagery, the same facts have a directly opposite meaning. As the Oxford physiologist and systems biologist Denis Noble points out, we could just as well write:

> [Genes] are trapped in huge colonies, locked inside highly intelligent beings, moulded by the outside world, communicating with it by complex processes, through which, blindly, as if by magic, function emerges. They are in you and me; we are the systems that allow their code to be read, and their preservation is totally dependent on the joy that we experience in reproducing ourselves. We are the ultimate rationale for their existence.   (2006: 12)

The whole message is in the rhetoric.

Units need not compete

What this shows is that we don't need drama here. We don't have to choose between units because selection can work at all levels. This emerged as, after a time, the claim that group selection was impossible began to look unconvincing. Today, as Sloan Wilson says, naive groupism is still a mistake but claims for group selection must be evaluated on a case-by-case basis, along with other evolutionary hypotheses. Cases have now been well verified, some of them involving bacteria, but others occurring in human life. And this raises a much bigger issue that affects the whole notion of what a unit is. If each group, as it becomes more unified, begins to act more like a unit itself, it becomes meaningless and arbitrary to pick out a single unit, such as gene, cell, individual or group, as more real than the others and to dramatise it as an agent controlling the rest. The cell biologist Lynn Margulis proposed this concept in the 1970s to explain the evolution of nucleated cells as symbiotic communities of bacterial cells. The concept was then generalized to explain other major transitions, from the origin of life as communities of cooperating molecular reactions to multicellular organisms and social insect colonies. Each unit plays its own part in selection at its own level; they are not in competition.

This has particularly interesting consequences for the human case because of the effects of culture. Among creatures that can talk, new attitudes or discoveries can spread incomparably faster than they can among those who depend on genetic mutation alone. This obvious fact has long led people to suggest that cultural evolution allows the inheritance of acquired characteristics. Biologists have often treated this point cautiously because they didn't want to sound Lamarckian but it is actually a crucial one. It means that human speech represents a whole new ball game for the working of group selection.

We tend to think first of how this would work in physical examples such as the invention of tools and weapons, but probably more central was the spread of cooperative social *attitudes*: the ways of living that made people more chatty, more open, more interested in each other's activities, more likely to learn by each other's examples. When we consider the huge range of differences that have actually grown up between human cultures, we surely have to think of this sort of learning as a central factor in human development. When we note how ready people in various cultures have often been to class foreigners with different habits as not being human at all, the great force of this influence becomes clear. In these cases cultural difference operates just like a species difference; indeed, it has been called "pseudo-speciation". And this means that it is a factor of the same order as a difference of genes.

This point may actually be relevant to the puzzle about how our ancestors managed to eliminate the apparently better-adapted

Neanderthals. It is now being suggested that perhaps *Homo sapiens*'s superiority lay simply in being better organized, better able to plan joint operations of a kind that never crossed the minds of their more solitary opponents. In fact, the development of what Darwin called the social instincts was central to their success.

3

The natural springs of morality

Intelligence and remorse

This determined hostility of biologists to group selection is just one expression of the gulf that has opened between Darwin's own approach and the social atomism preached by those who claim to be his followers: both the "social Darwinists" in his own day and the neo-Darwinists now. Social atomism is not really an essential part of the idea of evolution. It is essentially political: an ideology shaped by Enlightenment individualism, one that takes different forms according to the political and social pressures of the day. Its first strong expression was Hobbes's sharp reaction against religious wars and it still echoes the simplistic rhetoric of its founder. It is not interested in relating its findings to the emotional complexity of our actual lives. And, because it comes from a political context, it is habitually polemical, dealing in extremes. I shall try later to look at this very important element in our thought in its own terms and consider how we ought to use it.

But it needs to be kept separate from Darwin. He, by contrast, was trying to grasp how something as complex as actual human motivation – including moral sensibility – could possibly have evolved. He wanted to understand it ethologically, as an expression of the lifestyle of our species. And, unlike many people who attempt this, he did not simplify his task by reducing humans to stereotypical animals. He looked at both people and the various kinds of animals in their actual bewildering complexity. And he started his enquiry from one of the most puzzling human traits – morality – because he thought it so central.

As we have seen, in introducing this topic he remarked that "of all the differences between man and the lower animals, the moral sense or conscience is by far the most important". He noted the huge, disturbing question about how words such as *ought* get their authority, recognized that it has many aspects, but proposed to look at the light cast on it from one single angle that had so far been neglected – that of natural history. This he did, sketching out a wide background of social behaviour in other animals and explaining why he thought that any sociable creature that became highly intelligent would be forced by its increased intelligence to develop a morality. This follows, he says, from an individual's becoming aware of inner conflict:

> *Firstly*, the social instincts lead an animal to take pleasure in the society of its fellows and to feel sympathy with them, and to perform various services for them .... *Secondly*, as soon as the mental faculties had become highly developed, *images of all past actions and motives would be incessantly passing through the brain of each individual* and that feeling of dissatisfaction which invariably results ... from any unsatisfied instinct, would arise, as often as it was perceived that the enduring and always present social instinct had yielded to some other instinct, at the time stronger, but neither enduring in its nature nor leaving behind it a very vivid impression.
>
> (72, emphasis added)

Intelligence, in fact, is not just a useful calculating tool. It is also a light that comes on within us, a new kind of self-awareness that arises whether we ask for it or not. An intelligent agent's own past acts can now haunt him, confronting him with the clash between his own motives, asking him which of the conflicting wishes he really wants to identify with.

Darwin gives an illuminating instance of the difference that intelligence could make about this. Parent swallows, he says, often desert their young to join a migrating swarm because their strong urge to brood chicks is overwhelmed by the still stronger need to migrate. If, however, they had a sharper intelligence:

> when arrived at the end of her journey, and the migratory instinct ceases to act, what an agony of remorse each bird would feel, if, from being endowed with great mental activity, she could not prevent the image continually passing before her mind of her young ones perishing in the north from cold and hunger. (91)

And something like this is indeed, as he says, a frequent human situation:

> Man, from the activity of his mental faculties, cannot avoid reflection; past impressions and images are incessantly passing through his mind with distinctness .... (89)

> At the moment of action, man will no doubt be apt to follow the stronger impulse; and though this may occasionally prompt him to the noblest deeds, it will far more commonly lead him to gratify his own desire at the expense of other men. But after their gratification, when past and weaker impressions are contrasted with the ever-enduring social instincts,

> retribution will surely come. Man will then feel dissatisfied
> with himself, and will resolve with more or less force to act
> differently for the future. This is conscience, for conscience
> looks backwards and judges past actions, inducing that kind
> of dissatisfaction which, if weak, we call regret, and if severe,
> remorse. (91)

The central peculiarity of humans is *not*, then, just their improved power of calculation. It is their wider perspective, their more comprehensive viewpoint. They have a longer view backwards and forwards in life. Their increased power of reasoning is not just a pocket calculator; it is a general intensification of inner activity. Besides recalling isolated acts, these more thoughtful beings now see the continuous course of their own conduct and can compare it with that of others. They cannot always avoid thinking about these things and – because they have become aware of the reactions of those around them – they have to see them in part from the point of view of others. That is the context in which the question of judging particular acts begins to be important.

Nietzsche on the evolution of morals

It is interesting that Nietzsche, in one of his more helpful and constructive moods, gives a rather similar account of this invention. Starting the second essay of *On the Genealogy of Morals*, he writes: "To breed an animal *with the right to make promises* – is not this the paradoxical task that nature has set itself in the case of man?" The creation of such a creature is difficult, he says, because, in primitive life, it is very important to keep forgetting what is past as one moves on to whatever follows. Despite this:

this animal which needs to be forgetful, in which forgetting represents a force, a form of robust health, has bred in itself an opposing faculty, a memory, with the aid of which forgetfulness is abrogated in certain cases – namely in those cases where promises are made .... Man himself must first of all have become *calculable, regular, necessary*, even in his own image of himself if he is to be able to stand security for *his own future* ....

This precisely is the long story of how *responsibility* originated .... The tremendous labour of what I have called the "morality of mores" – the labour performed by man upon himself during the greater part of the existence of the human race, his entire *prehistoric* labour – finds in this its meaning, its great justification, notwithstanding the severity, tyranny, stupidity and idiocy involved in it: with the aid of the morality of mores and the social straitjacket man was actually *made* calculable. (Nietzsche 1969: 57–8)

Thus, like Darwin, Nietzsche fully saw the vital importance of this development. And he too located the impetus for it in the need for the *wholeness* of the personality: the desperate sense of wanting continuity through time that dawns on a creature as it becomes more and more aware of its past and future. Nietzsche also saw, like Darwin, that the consequence must be an endemic state of conflict:

Thus began the gravest and uncanniest illness, from which humanity has not yet recovered, man's suffering *of man, of himself* – the result of a forcible sundering from his animal past.

Let us add at once that, on the other hand, the existence on earth of an animal soul turned against itself ... was something so new, profound, unheard-of, enigmatic, contradictory and pregnant with a future that the aspect of the earth was essentially altered .... He gives rise to an interest, a hope, almost a certainty, as if with him something were announcing and preparing itself, as if man were not a goal but only a way, an episode, a bridge, a great promise. (*Ibid*.: 85)

As is well known, Nietzsche spent most of his life attacking that same "severity, tyranny, stupidity and idiocy" of which he had complained, things that have so often accompanied the "morality of custom" that it is impressive to find him doing such thorough justice here to the importance of the morality itself. And indeed, just after describing its development in this way, he insists on the need to travel beyond it:

At the end of this tremendous process, where the tree at last brings forth fruit .... we discover that the ripest fruit is the *sovereign individual*, like only to himself, liberated again from morality of custom, autonomous and supramoral ... and in him a proud consciousness, quivering in every muscle, of *what* has at length been achieved and become flesh in him, a consciousness of his own power and freedom, a sensation of mankind come to completion .... This emancipated individual with the actual right to make promises ... how should he not be aware of his own superiority over all those who lack the right to make promises and stand as their own guarantors? .... He is bound to reserve a kick for the feeble windbags who promise without the right to do so. (*Ibid*.: 59–60)

This, of course, is part of Nietzsche's well-known contribution to the individualistic tradition that is our main topic, and we shall come back to it later. If the kind of ethical caste system that he seems to propose here, allowing moral innovators – supermen – free licence to kick other people, surprises us it is worth while to remember that Nietzsche, unlike Hobbes, lived at a time when European civilization seemed secure and ossified, a time when civilized people, particularly in his native Germany, were complacent and sure that nothing need change. His main message to them was the drastic need for change. And it is hard to keep that sense in balance with a full appreciation of the timeless, indispensable background of shared customs.

Rationality and sanity

To return, however, to Darwin, anyone used to philosophical discussions of moral issues will find it striking that Darwin sees no need to call in Reason here as an independent assessor. Unlike Kant and many other moralists, he does not treat it as an external arbiter, a power set over against the whole range of feelings, having the right to determine final choice. Quite differently, he suggests that, once the conflict is perceived, it is something in the social motives themselves that often gives them the right to prevail. And conscience – the faculty that has to decide these questions – is not a distinct professional judge inside each one of us but an aspect of the whole person who deals with the conflict: a unifying entity who had never before appeared on this stage.

What kind of authority, then, does conscience have? The affections that the impulsive act has wounded are, he says – unlike the impulse – "ever-enduring", chronic rather than acute. But why does ever-enduringness give them a special status? Because, as Darwin suggests, it means they are a deeper, more integral part of our nature. They are something more central to our characters than the passing impulses that often overwhelm them. It is not mere chance that makes them keep surfacing in our lives. They are persistent because they do something crucial for us. *They are the organs that show us that we really are not alone*, the channels through which we perceive the reality of those we love. It is through them that we grasp the otherness of others. And, even though we so often ignore these messages, without that assurance we cannot live.

Is this right? Some critics suspect that it is all too chancy, that it depends too much on our happening to be members of a particular species. Thus Kant wrote:

> We should not dream for a moment of trying to derive the reality of this principle [duty] from the special characteristics of human nature. For duty has to be a practical, unconditioned necessity of action; it must therefore hold for all rational beings ... only because of this can it also be a law for all human wills. (Kant 1997: 88)

In this spirit we might, of course, ask: if, instead of being mammals, we were alien beings who did not have these feelings, would we then still have these duties? Kant thought that we still would, because he believed the authority of morals was independent of all feelings, arising simply from rationality – from a rational being's recognition that all other rational beings have unconditional value:

> All the objects of inclination have only a conditional value; for if there were not these inclinations and the needs grounded on them, their objects would be valueless. Inclinations themselves, as sources of needs, are so far from having an absolute value to make them desirable for their own sake that it must rather be the universal wish of every rational being to be wholly free from them. (*Ibid.*: 90)

What, then, would be the situation of rational beings who just happened to have no feelings at all, or only destructive ones?

What, for instance, about Mephistopheles in Goethe's *Faust*, who declares:

> I am the spirit who always says No.
> And rightly too, for all that comes to birth
> Is fit for overthrow, as nothing worth;
> Wherefore the world were better sterilized;
> Thus all that's here as evil recognized
> Is gain to me, and downfall, ruin, sin
> The very element I prosper in.
>
> (*Faust, Part 1*: scene iii, 73–9)

This may be a consistent attitude, but is it a rational one? Or does rationality perhaps involve something more than consistency?

In common life, *rationality* does not mean just cognitive neatness. We are not likely to call somebody rational who reasons consistently from premises like these. The same doubt arises about single-minded fanatics even when their chosen maxim is one that we actually approve of. We may well think these people insane or sociopathic, and those conditions are not thought to be compatible with rationality.

The value of mutual dependence

Would things be any better if these beings had no feelings at all? Kant seems to suggest – as the Stoics had done – that that would indeed be an ideal state because inclinations indicate needs, which are marks of imperfection. But, without any needs or inclinations, how could action ever start at all? Nor do we actually think that apathy – a lack of inclinations – is any sign of rationality. (Mr Spock of *Star Trek* is not really a counter-example here; he clearly has all the normal human feelings.)

What Kant and the Stoics have missed is that our need for each other – our need for all the normal intercourse of human life – is not a weakness but a strength. It is our lifeline, our essential passport to the real world. It is what points us outward to all the riches around us, the great stores of *otherness* in which we need to live. Of course our dependencies are dangerous, but who wants to live safely like a billiard ball or a doll that never leaves its package? Of course the Enlightenment message about the need to be adult – to take full responsibility for our own lives – is a sound one. But to exaggerate it into a rejection of all dependence is to lose touch with the human situation altogether. If we try to do that, we lose as adults the vital, realistic sense of our entirely dependent situation that we gained as small children. We then risk ceasing to be properly human at all.

Yet the idea that all feelings, and particularly feelings of dependence, are simply weaknesses has been curiously strong in our tradition. It is related to the Greek notion that feelings are something alien and invasive, things that happen to us rather than activities. The Greek word *pathos*, latinized as *passio*, means an experience that we passively undergo. Thought, by contrast, is viewed as an activity under our control and therefore more dignified.

But our underlying acceptance of values – our love of the people and places and causes that we mind about and our commitment to them – is not something passive, not something imposed from outside. It is an active policy, a lasting decision to aim our activity in certain ways. Love and hatred are not mere opinions, they are feelings, but feelings do not just happen to us, like a stroke or a fit of sneezing. Any feelings that last longer than a mere instantaneous impulse become parts of our thought and – unless we reject them – they determine its direction.

This means that the ordinary idea of rationality is not just one of intellectual power or consistency but includes *aims*: desires and wishes that are recognizably human. And Kant, while allowing a very wide range for the possible aims of rational beings, surely took this condition for granted like the rest of us. He assumes, for instance, that these beings will value each other because consistency demands that they should do so if they value themselves. But suppose they do not value themselves, or do not do so for the right sorts of reasons? Suppose they are consumed by self-hatred, or are already considering suicide?

It is not, I suggest, just an accident that all those we think of as typical rational beings – namely human ones – have begun their lives as babies, living in a deeply affectionate and dependent relationship with those who reared them. They are shaped for life by that relation, even though, in later life, they may try to forget it and avoid acknowledging any kind of dependence. As far as we know, this background seems to be necessary to lead a creature to take others seriously enough to communicate with them at all. Doing this means seeing them as, in some sense, equals and ends in themselves.

Bees and other alien species

What, however, about alien beings? Following up his suggestion about a hypothetical species that might become moral because it had become intelligent, Darwin suggests an interesting parallel:

> In the same manner as various animals have some sense of beauty, though they admire widely different objects, so they might have a sense of right and wrong, though led by it to follow different lines of conduct. If, for instance, … men were reared under precisely the same conditions as hive-bees, there can hardly be a doubt that our unmarried females would, like the worker-bees, think it a sacred duty to kill their brothers, and mothers would strive to kill their fertile daughters, and

no-one would think of interfering. Nevertheless the bee, or any other social animal, would in our supposed case gain, as it appears to me, some feeling of right and wrong, or a conscience. There would often be a struggle and ... an inward monitor would tell the animal that it would have been better to have followed the one course than the other. (73)

Obviously, however, this destructiveness would be balanced in the bee by deep loyalty and affection for its fellows, which would (again) be appropriate to the care it had received in infancy. Those feelings would have to supply the strong social motive that would activate its conscience. It is also possible, of course, that this kind of destructiveness would actually prevent bees, or bee-like creatures, from developing rationality at all. We know, after all, that human destructiveness stands in the way of human rationality and limits its scope.

Darwin points out that the particular repertoire of natural feelings from which a species starts can always pose grave problems in this way to the project of harmonization. In the human case he instances particularly the partiality of our affections, which so often blocks our attempts at justice. Yet, as he notes, this partiality is often balanced by a sense of fairness, which is also natural, one which, again, we share with other advanced social species and that has often had great influence. But for earthly creatures, as opposed to abstract minds or computers, the direct personal affection in early youth on which our partiality centres is the irreplaceable focus of all further development.

Swallows too, like most other birds, are, of course, emotionally formed by these strong bonds of affection uniting parents and young, just as mammals are. Mammals and birds share this emotional structure, even though they are not at all closely related, having in fact no common ancestry nearer than quite primitive reptiles. This is one of many interesting cases of evolutionary convergence: the development of similar features by unrelated organisms in response to situations when their needs become similar. Stephen Jay Gould drew attention to such cases in *The Panda's Thumb*. Conway Morris, however, has emphasized their significance in a much more interesting way. They show, he says, that, at many points in evolution, only one possible path of further development actually makes sense. That path will therefore be taken by all species that arrive at this juncture, despite their very different starting-points, even though alternative routes may seem to be available. Unlike Gould, who thought that in principle anything can happen in evolution, Conway Morris therefore proposes that social creatures, and eventually intelligent ones such as humans, were bound to develop.

If that is right, it suggests that the only way in which creatures could have gained high intelligence was the way in which they actually did do so – namely, in the context of strong natural affections. They might then indeed, as Darwin suggests, have developed it largely as a solution to the problems that those affections pose when they conflict, that is, to the social problems posed by living cooperatively together. Looked at from that angle, human thought and human feeling do not just happen to be housemates; they are mutually dependent elements in an organic whole.

This is very different from traditional stories about the sources of human intelligence. As Nicholas Humphrey observes, "fifteen years ago, nothing in the text-books about human evolution referred to man's need to do psychology; the talk was all of tool-making, spear-throwing and fire-lighting – practical rather than social intelligence" (1986: 40). Humphrey himself has been largely responsible for shifting the focus here by concentrating on the social role that intelligence plays in the life of other creatures. Observing gorillas, he was struck by the apparent discrepancy between their known intelligence and the apparent easiness of their lives. What, he asked, was all this intelligence for? In their natural surroundings they seemed to do nothing much except eat and sleep. What evolutionary pressures, then, had made these large brains develop? Pondering this, Humphrey gradually became aware of what were the real difficulties of their lives – namely problems arising from their personal relations:

> The reason why life in the forest seemed to pose so few problems for these apes is precisely because the gorilla *family*, as a unit, is so well adapted to it ....
>
> The social life of a gorilla may not, to an outsider, look all that problematical, but that is only because the animals themselves are so accomplished at it. None the less there *are* endless small disputes ....
>
> Major set-tos may not happen often, but when they do they can be literally a matter of life and death ... The intelligence required to survive socially is something of quite a different order from that required to cope with the material world.
>
> (1986: 37–9)

Who, then, is this person Reason?

Our intellectual and emotional faculties are not, then, distinct commodities, bought separately like chalk and cheese and competing to control us. They are interdependent aspects of a single constitution. This is also true of the other more-or-less intelligent creatures with which we are acquainted. We cannot, therefore, easily guess what would happen to a hypothetical species that might take the quite different path of developing theoretical reason alone, as has often been suggested.

This makes it hard to explain conscience or reason in Kant's way as essentially an intellectual faculty, independent of species-specific feelings. Of course the idea of a direct conflict between reason and feeling is familiar to us because our tradition often does treat reason as something distinct from the feelings that resist it. And this is a natural way of talking because so much of our experience revolves around fairly simple conflicts. Indeed, Plato's image in the *Phaedrus* of Reason as a charioteer trying desperately to drive an ill-matched pair of horses tells a story that sounds familiar to us. Yet we need to look harder at this kind of imagery.

We need to ask, for instance, what are this charioteer's own aims and motives? What does *he* mind about? Where is he going so enthusiastically? He is evidently not an impartial computer, so what are his values? In the myth, he is driving his chariot through the heavens, following his own tutelary god, on his way to see the sublime mysteries that will enlighten his life. He is there, in fact, to grasp the highest ideals. And, as Plato makes clear, both here and in the *Republic*, this charioteer stands simply for the intellectual part of the soul (*to logistikon*; *Republic* 439d). He alone knows where he is going and why he must go there. The feelings are just his horses, some of which obstruct him terribly while others help him. They are simply sources of power, not of insight.

But is it possible to represent the way we perceive our ideals – our values – as something purely intellectual like this, without explaining how this insight involves love? Aristotle was surely right to say rather that "intellect itself moves nothing, but only the intellect which aims at an end and is practical". This, he says, can be called either desiring reason or reasoning desire – "And such a cause of action is a man" (*Nicomachean Ethics* 1139a–b). In short, the sharp division between thought and emotion really doesn't work at this point. We need to drop it and talk of the whole person.

It is noticeable that when we speak of *reason* as opposing feeling in ordinary life, what we mean is not usually pure intellectual consistency. It is rather a combination of several other motives: background ones, which we think highly of, which normally move us strongly but are taken for granted. These motives may centre on prudence, force of habit and a general consideration for others – in short, the kind of thing that Darwin called "the social instincts". They may also concern some general cause that is now important to us. But they have to be there. In states of depression, when they may lapse, action merely becomes impossible.

It makes sense to call this collection of motives *reason* because they are organized. They form a pattern, a background system that we are accustomed to refer to when we start thinking. By contrast, the new, interfering motive that contends against them – perhaps anger, ambition, pity or love – is a sudden interloper, an isolated force opposing a general policy. Thus the reminder that calls us to resist this interloper may well be expressed by saying "be reasonable", "stop and think". But we don't understand this just as advice to make our thought more consistent. We accept it as the voice of this well-known collection of background motives. We know that consistency with it will take us back to our central life policy, which is indeed something rationally considered. But unless its aims are ones that we still mind about, consistency with it will not move us to action.

Kant, when he insisted that "reason can itself be practical" surely meant by it this kind of complex of considered convictions charged with emotive force, however far that combination may have travelled from the raw motives that first contributed to it. This is what, in his view, brings it about that rational beings mind about each other: that they naturally reverence other rational beings and see them all as existing as ends in themselves, not just as convenient means to further each one's own ends. Thus, for him as well as Plato, rationality clearly has affective elements, ones that go far beyond mere consistent calculation.

Philosophers, however, have always tended to personify Reason as a separate, authoritative character in the drama, a corrective power set over against all feeling. Plato's charioteer is not interested in understanding what his horses want. He just wants to make them go his way. Pascal, who wrote that "the heart has reasons of which reason knows nothing", may sound more sympathetic to the emotions, but he still makes no suggestion about how to understand them. Instead, he makes these two characters sound like an ill-matched married couple, so resigned to not understanding each other that they no longer even try to communicate, except perhaps by notes ("Baker calls Thursday"). But how, we may ask, has Reason got itself into this isolated predicament? And if it has, what is its authority?

4

Coming to terms with Reason

The revolt of the passions

It is not surprising that, after much talk of this kind, Hume grew tired of the drama where Reason was in charge and decided to reverse the plot, putting feeling on top instead. He protested that "We speak not strictly and philosophically when we talk of the combat of passion and of reason. *Reason is, and ought only to be, the slave of the passions* and can never pretend to any other office than to serve and obey them" (1978: bk II, §3, 415). Thought, said Hume, has no motive force on its own; it is a purely cognitive power, concerned solely with the discovery of truth and falsehood. "The passions" – the feelings – are the only forces that can actually move people.

This is well worth saying. Yet it is still just one more divisive pattern of the kind that has attracted theorists for so long. It still posits an incurable split between two aspects of the human psyche. This gulf may be located between theory and practice, or between "hard" and "soft" thinking, or again between the arts and the sciences, between facts and values, between objective and subjective, between science and religion or even between men and women (as Tennyson put it in *The Princess* [line 430], "Man with the head and woman with the heart"). But wherever they put their gulf, philosophers are strongly inclined to take sides about it.

Hume's reverse formulation of the drama does have the virtue of protesting against the earlier exaltation of thought over feeling. And in his *Enquiry Concerning the Principles of Morals* he does indeed develop a much more positive view than any of his predecessors did about natural human tendencies to goodness. In fact, he paves the way for Darwin's later developments. But his formula only gives us a change of despot, not an improved constitution. By still treating Reason as an isolated factor he perpetuates the unrealistic opposition between it and feeling of every kind. Like his rationalist opponents, he still ignores the wide central area of *attitudes*, life-positions that involve both these elements. Thus he rules that the source of morality is something he calls the "sentiment of humanity", an emotion that leads us to respect other human beings. This motive, he says:

> recommends the same object to general approbation, and makes every man, or most men, agree in the same opinion or decision respecting it ... The other passions produce in every breast many strong sentiments of desire or aversion; but these are neither felt so much in common, nor are so comprehensive, as to be the foundation of any general system and established theory of blame or approbation ....
>
> The humanity of one man is the humanity of every one, and the same object touches the passion in all human creatures.
>
> (Section IX, pt. 1, para. 221)

This is an attractive idea. But the notion that a single "sentiment" could produce this wide agreement and acquire this authority is not realistic. It is not really plausible to describe so general an attitude as just one feeling among others, comparing it, say, to fear or ambition.

To become general and effective it needs a great deal of thought, and that thought is just what gives it authority, distinguishing it (as he explains) from "the other passions".

Terry Eagleton explains both the strengths and the drawbacks of Hume's position and of the Enlightenment ethic behind it well:

> We would not expect an affable bourgeois like David Hume to defend a conception of selfless sacrifice – one which involves the more austere, traumatic, death-dealing virtues, but which exists in the name of a more copious life all round ... All this strikes him as morbid and masochistic, as it does the conventional liberal wisdom of our own time .... It is true that the good life is all about grace, ease and well-being, as these Enlightenment thinkers grasped in their own way .... What they could not see from their historical vantage-point was that to achieve such a condition requires from time to time the sombre revolutionary virtues of sacrifice and self-discipline.
>
> (2009: 60)

In fact, thought – hard, troublesome thought – is needed as well as feeling. And Hume's sharp, simple division between Reason and Feeling still ignores the many kinds of thought by which people struggle to find their way between wild emotion at one extreme and pure abstract calculation at the other. It ignores reflection, rumination, contemplation, brooding, worrying, dreaming, reminiscing, speculating, considering and imagining. In particular, it ignores that deliberate redirecting of attention by which we can, if we please, gradually transform our feelings. Sustained attention to someone's faults can easily harden a passing fit of anger into hatred. Equally, sustained attention to their good qualities can transform it into respect.

These are the kinds of processes by which we form the general life-policy that guides us when (as just mentioned) we try to "be reasonable". It is through their continued working that we manage to change and develop that policy when we see its faults. Explicit, articulate argument is just the last stage in that long creative process, one that becomes possible only when we have finally come to "see things differently". And even then it often involves us in distracting controversies that are already going on outside us.

Hume, however, wasn't interested in these paths by which we constantly try to make sense of our raw feelings. Similarly Kant, accepting the same sharp cleavage between reason and feeling, wasn't interested in the affective element that is needed to determine the *direction* of even our most abstract value-judgments. He took it for granted that rational beings would be in favour of other rational beings – would care positively about them – rather than preferring to get rid of them, like Mephistopheles. Yet we know that there are indeed people – we call them psychopaths – who seem to be perfectly intelligent, but who act without any regard to other people's interests. Indeed, if asked, they may say that these do not matter at all. They may not be dedicated, like Mephistopheles, to general destruction – in fact they are not likely to be dedicated to any cause – but they genuinely lack, and will sometimes explicitly reject, the sense that others are of value. Intelligent though they are, argument does not shift them from this position.

On the other hand, there are also people who have genuine spasms of sympathetic feeling – who at times are horrified to hear of suffering – but who don't generalize that horror to include the sufferings of people they don't like, or to times when they don't feel sympathy. This defect can be called sentimentality, narrowness, prejudice or lack of imagination, but it clearly isn't an incapacity to feel.

Propaganda problems

Thus, as is perfectly well known, neither thought nor feeling on its own can generate the kind of moral attitude that exists in even the most basic of human communities. (Even the Mafia has its own moral code.) To produce this, the two factors must work together; they are inseparable. Yet philosophers have often treated them as competitors. Kant's successors have largely abandoned his faith in an all-explaining Reason but they have continued his feud against views (such as emotivism) that lay more stress on feeling. In recent times, English-speaking philosophers have treated this opposition as a battle between rationalists and empiricists, seeing it as part of a wider epistemological debate about rival sources of knowledge – reason versus experience – a contest that, it seemed, one side might hope eventually to win.

By contrast, what the great philosophers of the past usually wanted was primarily to change the world. Their interest was not in contrasting various forms of moral judgement but in using all human faculties to bring about a better way of living. Plato, for instance, did not think of reasoning primarily as formal calculation but as a spiritual activity, a practice that could take a man above the delusive tangles of the world and show him the eternal truths. He thought that hard study, especially mathematical study, was needed for this and was therefore needed both for individual and political salvation. So he urged people to follow the intellectual life, but only because of its place in spiritual life as a whole.

Thus, starting from Socrates' fairly general idea that "the unexamined life is unlivable to man" he ended up campaigning for a very special intellectual way of living that implied a special kind of politics. His *Republic* is obviously meant to be a profoundly revolutionary document and has indeed had huge effects in real life, not least in giving serious academic work the high prestige that it has had ever since. Similarly, Kant was much concerned to resist the romantic *Sturm und Drang* movement active in his day, which exalted the value of feeling over reason, not just in theory but in practice too.

Epicurus, by contrast, saw the good life very differently. He thought that study simply distracts us from the kinds of satisfaction that we really need. "Set your sail; O happy youth, and flee from every form of education" was his advice. Similarly Hume, having described the puzzles in which persistent thought involves us, advised us to take frequent breaks from it:

> Most fortunately it happens that, since reason is incapable of dispelling these clouds, Nature herself suffices to that purpose, and cures me of this philosophical melancholy and delirium, either by relaxing this bent of mind, or by some avocation, and lively impression of my senses, which obliterate all these chimeras. I dine, I play a game of backgammon, I converse and am merry with my friends; and when, after three or four hours amusement I would return to these speculations, they appear so cold, and strained, and ridiculous that I cannot find it in my heart to enter into them further.   (1978: vol. 1, pt iv, §7, 254)

This, too, has wider consequences. Hume does not just think that philosophers should sometimes take time off from their work but that all of us should be extremely cautious about applying reasoning to life at all, especially any reasoning – like that in the *Republic* or *Das Kapital* – that might invite us to change the world. Although he delighted in argument, he had, at a deep level, little confidence in the application of abstract reason to life and a strong sense of the danger of doctrinaire politics. He thought tradition was a much safer guide, and accordingly he wrote persuasive and popular history from a conservative viewpoint.

In this way, philosophical discussions about the parts played by reason and feeling in morality have repeatedly dramatised the issue to recommend particular ways of life. Instead of trying to understand the connection between these two essential elements, sages have taken sides between them and exaggerated the conflict. That fractiousness is particularly unfortunate on this subject because personal identity is an issue that directly affects us all. Emphasis on the division encourages readers to accept this clash as incurable rather than trying to restore continuity between the different sides of their nature. They tend to suppose that the problem is rather like that of keeping their hobbies separate from their work. Perhaps they can think on Sundays and can just feel the rest of the time. Or they can think in the university and feel when they get home.

Possible self-unifying strategies

There is, of course, a genuine difficulty here about bringing together our ideas of thought and feeling, a difficulty about how we should envisage our nature as a whole. The mere fact that we are so constantly involved in conflict stirs up trouble here, and debates between different philosophers have undoubtedly increased it. In this difficulty, Darwin's evolutionary approach to the problem is surely extremely helpful. By pointing out how much friendly order and cooperation – how much, indeed, of what we call humanity – there already is in the lives of other social animals, he undermines the notion that our own "animal nature" is something alien and unmanageable. And he shows how, in each species, thought and feeling are adapted to work together.

How then should we conceive of these inner conflicts? Perhaps a helpful image, even if not a very exciting one, might be that of a committee: a committee whose members know each other well, and also know that, in the end, they will actually have to agree on some sort of decision. Of course these members can, if they like, just go on being awkward and make business impossible. This is indeed what our inner arguers often do when we are children, and some people never get beyond it. Most of us, however, get a little better at compromise as time goes on, and begin trying to balance the different aims that our various wishes are presenting more effectively.

On good days, we can think through a solution that does some justice to all these aims and feel tolerably satisfied with it. And even when things go less well, we know that we can still go on working on this inner dialectic, trying to get something that will count as a decision of the whole person. In this process all the various members learn something and the "whole person" who, it emerges, has become a slightly different one from the person who started.

That whole person is, as I just mentioned, a crucial character in the drama, even though it is often shadowy and hard to find. No authoritative outside adjudicator called Reason can stand in for it. The word, "reasoning" simply describes the process of bringing our conflicting motives together, weighing them and trying to combine them to the satisfaction of our whole being. The motives themselves – even when they are very general ones such as prudence or curiosity – are still feelings, not just thoughts. They are, in fact, what Darwin called *the social instincts*: natural wishes and fears that flow from our emotional constitution, shaped and educated by our own life and our tradition. Our aim is always to bring them together in a way that makes sense to the whole.

Does this rather administrative image seem unsatisfactory? One reason for doubts may be that we are uneasy with compromise. We would like something more authoritative and final. That is surely what has made the idea of enthroning Reason as the judge so attractive, and what makes even Hume's picture of the Sentiment of Humanity producing universal agreement seem tidier. This, however, is surely one of the points at which we cannot avoid a kind of pluralism, an admission that the truth has many aspects, between which we must sometimes choose. Our nature really is too complex, and our lives too muddled, for us to be sure of clear solutions. Yet we know, both from our own past experience and from history, that continued efforts at compromise can always improve things and can sometimes make difficulties vanish altogether.

Are we animals after all?

Another source of alarm, however, is the limited membership of our consultative committee. We may have secured agreement among our own natural motives, but is this enough when those motives are said to be, in some sense, of the same kind as those of other animals? Do we not need some outside pope, or some official, separate oracle within us, to validate these verdicts? This thought is surely what alarms many people about Darwin's dictum that "the difference in mind between man and the higher animals, great as it is, is certainly one of degree and not of kind" (105).

How we understand this remark depends, first, on how sensitive we happen to be feeling about species prestige and then on what we mean by a difference in kind. On the first point, Darwin has conceded that importing intelligence into a given emotional constitution does indeed change its nature hugely. By making self-criticism possible it throws a different light on everything, allowing all sorts of wider judgements. The feelings that develop after this will not be the same as the feelings that were present before it. Yet this change still has to be continuous with previous developments. It does not involve replacing our whole population of motives by newly designed substitutes. He goes on at once to explain how he conceives the different elements that will undergo this change:

81

We have seen that the senses and intuitions, the various emotions and faculties, such as love, memory, attention, curiosity, imitation, reason etc. of which man boasts, may be found in an incipient, or even in a well-developed condition, in the lower animals .... If it be maintained that certain powers, such as self-consciousness, abstraction etc. are peculiar to man, it may well be that these are the incidental results of other highly-advanced intellectual faculties; and these again are mainly the result of the continued use of a highly developed language. *At what age does the new-born infant possess the power of abstraction or become self-conscious and reflect on its own existence? We cannot answer, nor can we answer in regard to the ascending organic scale ...*

(105–6, emphasis added)

We can't indeed, but this often doesn't seem to have been recognized. It is worth while at this point to notice the extraordinary confidence with which writers in our tradition still claim to know for certain that non-human animals lack particular kinds of insight and may even be quite unconscious. Thus Nicholas Humphrey, despite his sensibility to gorillas' social life, says flatly that, at any "lower" stage, there is simply no inner life going on at all:

The great apes we can be fairly sure of, perhaps whales as well. Yet *Descartes was as nearly right as makes no matter* [in claiming that animals were automata]. If we walk down an English country lane, we walk by ourselves. Trees, birds, bees, the rabbit darting down its hole, the cow heavy with milk waiting at the farmer's gate, are all *as without insight into their condition as the dummies on show at Madame Tussaud's.*

(1986: 84, emphasis added)

Who is conscious?

Humphrey's only evidence for this is that dogs apparently fail a test of "self-knowledge", a test that involves noticing a mark painted on one's face when one sees it in a mirror. Since dogs, unlike primates and birds, are not primarily visual but attend chiefly to other senses such as smell, this is not surprising. In fact, to rely on this test is rather like proving humans to be stupid by showing that they fail to notice an unfamiliar scent.

Humphrey has, it seems, actually owned a dog for fourteen years (why keep one if it is only an automaton?) and he comments kindly, "sometimes I do not doubt that he is conscious. But is he?" He doesn't say whether the dog asks itself this same question about him. He would, he says, only accept that the dog is conscious if it passed the paint-spot exam, which it doesn't. But he has surely over-looked a much more obvious test, namely the one provided by those fourteen years. The sort of trials that face a dog attempting to live with humans are not easier than the trials a gorilla faces in living with a family of gorillas; the species difference makes them harder. Dogs can deal with these problems because, like their wolf ancestors and like ourselves, they are intensely sociable: that is, they attend constantly to those around them, care about them and are skilled at interpreting their behaviour. That is why they have been able to function since the earliest times as a fully integrated part of human life. (The dummies at Madame Tussaud's do not do these things, which is why people do not often keep them as pets).

Debates about these topics always get entangled in doubts about the role of language because some people seem to believe it is impossible to think without words. This idea can be pretty briskly refuted by attending to our frequent difficulty in finding the words to express our thoughts, or indeed by observing the behaviour of babies. Besides this, however, the suggestion is evolutionarily quite implausible. That we should suddenly have leapt from a totally thoughtless state to becoming able to think just at the point when our larynxes fitted us to talk makes no sense at all. And ever since we have started to talk, we have been using parts of our brains for that purpose which other species still have and which they put to other uses, most probably uses connected with understanding and communication. What are they doing with them now?

These are faculties that they clearly still have, even when we cannot penetrate them. What, for instance, is going on in the minds of elephants when they repeatedly visit the bones of their dead friends and often carry them about? Or how do they communicate – as they clearly do – over considerable distances? How, too, have they (like dogs) communicated so successfully with people during the long ages since they were first domesticated? Could dummies have done that?

Humphrey knows, of course, that his ruling about Madame Tussaud's will surprise people and, to pre-empt their complaints, he uses a special tone of bland incredulity, a tone that is familiar because it was regularly used until lately in the parallel case of human infants. Fifty years ago, learned persons constantly assured parents that their babies had no real mental life; in particular, that if they ever seemed to smile before they were three months old this could only be due to wind. The burden of proof was always on those who claimed communication here, and no proof was ever deemed adequate to meet the demand. Since that time, of course, observers who take the trouble to attend to small children have uncovered an immense range of sensitive and intelligent behaviour: uncovered it, that is, in the sense of revealing it to the learned world, which alone had so far refused to recognize it. No reason has ever been given why the previous confident negative belief was ever held.

Child psychologists who were interested in making this advance had to face down a special kind of embarrassment that can afflict scholars when they are asked to attend to everyday domestic topics. This embarrassment has also been a central trouble about animals, especially domesticated ones. Part of the reason why Darwin's work on *The Expression of the Emotions* has never had the attention that it deserves is undoubtedly that it was embarrassing in both these ways, dealing with animals – often with domestic ones simply because these provide clear and handy examples – and also with human infants. His methods, too, differed from those of the present day in that he readily drew evidence from people outside the lab, who spent their working lives dealing with particular animals – people therefore who could not afford to misunderstand them – rather than relying on control experiments such as the paint-spot one, devised by scientists who dream up immensely general questions and decide to consider them settled by an arbitrarily chosen test. It is surely strange that many people now consider the paint-spot method to be the more scientific.

This kind of embarrassment about studying the familiar has continued to dog both these kinds of enquiry. When animal behaviour studies did eventually become accepted as scientific, academics still preferred to study exotic creatures such as wolves, meerkats or chimpanzees. It was a long time before the exceptionally interesting kind of inter-species communication that goes on between humans and domestic creatures was considered worthy of study at all, and it still has not had the attention it deserves.

Continuity and wholeness

Darwin, however, was remarkably free from this kind of embarrassment. When he has traced the continuities that link the human mind with its predecessors, as just noted, he goes on to describe the gradual steps by which our species may have found it possible to move from one level to the other:

The social instincts, which no doubt were acquired by man, as by the lower animals, for the good of the community, will from the first have given him some wish to aid his fellows, and some feeling of sympathy. Such impulses will have served him at a very early period as a rule of right and wrong. But as man gradually advanced in intellectual power and was enabled to trace the more remote consequences of his actions; as he acquired sufficient knowledge to reject baneful customs and superstitions; as he regarded more and more not only the welfare but the happiness of his fellow-men; as from habit, following on beneficial experience, instruction and example, his sympathies became more tender and widely diffused, so as to extend to the men of all races, to the imbecile, the maimed, and other useless members of society, and finally to the lower animals – so would the standard of his morality rise higher and higher ....

The ennobling belief in God is not universal with man; and the belief in active spiritual agencies naturally flows from his other mental powers.   (103–6)

And, as we have seen, he finally reaches his rather striking, and quite non-reductive, conclusion that:

the social instincts – the prime principle of man's moral constitution – with the aid of active intellectual; powers and the effects of habit, naturally lead to the golden rule, "As ye would that men should do to you do ye to them likewise", and this is the foundation of morality.   (106)

Thus he is equally convinced that the *elements* of morality have remained similar, having developed continuously out of their animal predecessors, and that the whole that they now form is indeed something seriously different. It may seem that calling this difference in mind between humans and other creatures "one of degree and not of kind" is a rather one-sided way of describing this complex situation. But, of course, Darwin had good reason for that emphasis. He needed to hammer home a point that was – and still is – utterly unwelcome to powerful parts of our tradition; namely, that there is nothing wrong with our emotional life being closely akin to that of other animals.

The other half of his dialectic – the excellence and distinctiveness of human institutions, especially morality – doesn't, of course, need champions. It has long been accepted and celebrated, indeed, in Western culture humanism often amounts to the worship of humanity. Several of its exponents, such as Auguste Comte and Julian Huxley, have explicitly promoted it as a religion. What is hard – perhaps impossible – is to bring this sense of human specialness into relation with our present evolutionary beliefs without altering our traditional beliefs about the lives of other animals. Even people who haven't the slightest intention of referring to God often become as uneasy as T. H. Huxley did when they try to bridge this gap and begin to look for help from outside. They still suspect that, as Kant put it, "we should not dream for a moment of trying to derive the reality of this principle (duty) from the special characteristics of human nature" (1997: 18).

But these *special characteristics of human nature* surely include the peculiar kind of intellect that our species owns. They include, in fact, our earthly brand of rationality. As we now know, even Euclidean mathematics, which used to be considered wholly universal, is only one possible system among many that can follow from adopting different axioms. The dispositions that go with our social nature are not, however, something that we can change when we fancy it, as we might our mathematical axioms. Being an essential aspect of who we are, they supply indispensable premises for our reasoning.

If we ever have to transact business with alien species, our moral relations with them will surely depend entirely on their having this same sort of rationality that we do, one that arises out of a similar emotional constitution – a rationality that starts from the premise that others matter, a premise we derive from love in our early childhood. In fact, unwelcome though the example may be, this is what already happens in our dealings with the many earthly creatures that we have successfully fitted into our lives. The animals that humans have managed to domesticate are necessarily all mammals or birds from species that already have a strong innate social structure that centres on regard for relatives, but is not confined to it. This strong sociability is particularly marked in dogs and horses, which are particularly renowned for the loyalty they show to their human companions, a loyalty that, as many people have remarked, can produce the same behaviour as conscious human virtue.

When Swift depicted his supposedly admirable and rational horses in *Gulliver's Travels*, he described them as coldly unconcerned about their relatives. This, however, only made them sound coldly unconcerned about everything, quite unlike real horses. Similarly, science fiction writers have often tried to depict beings guided solely by cognitive intellect, but they don't usually manage to make them very convincing.

Their attempt is, no doubt, usually designed as an argument against the partiality that, as we well know, is the downside of our strong attachment to relatives. Horror at this partiality was what made both Kant and the Stoics emphasize Reason so strongly. It was also what made Plato demand in the *Republic* that children should be communally nurtured, not even knowing who their real parents were. But attempts to homogenize babies in this way have always failed dismally because the babies themselves won't accept them. It turns out that strong individual attachments are an indispensable matrix for human sociability.

Moreover, the demand for fairness and justice rather than partiality is itself also a natural human feeling, as can be seen both from its prominence in all human institutions and, even more convincingly, from the determined way in which small children assert it. This egalitarian spirit constantly engages in debate against our narrowness at every human level from the playground on. That sense of fairness is also now being detected in other species by those who are, somewhat belatedly, now looking for such things experimentally.

On being evolved yet human

This, in fact, is surely one of many cases where nature itself sets up a dialectic, endowing us with feelings that are bound to conflict and also with powers of reconciling them. Darwin's point was that the capacities by which we seek a higher synthesis for these conflicts – and sometimes find it – are still parts of our evolved nature, as much parts of it as the simpler faculties that we share with other animals. This is surely right, and it does not mean that they have somehow lost their value or significance.

Unfortunately, however, both Darwin's supposed supporters and his opponents have often concluded that it does and that Darwin said so. Thus Le Fanu, discussing today's orthodoxy, which he attributes entirely to Darwin, writes that this:

> prevailing scientific view maintains that man's sense of himself as an autonomous independent being is no more than an illusion generated by his brain, and the joys and agonies of human love no more than a device for the propagation of his genes ... Together with Marx and Freud, [Darwin] is one of that triumvirate of imaginative thinkers of the nineteenth and

early twentieth centuries whose assertion of the priority of
the scientific view would occupy the centre stage of Western
thought for so long .... (2009: 250)

"Darwin made theological and spiritual explanations of life
superfluous" as Douglas Futuyma of the University of New
York observes. (*Ibid.*: 261)

But Darwin never asserted any such general priority of "the
scientific view" – meaning presumably the view of the natural
sciences – over, say, the historical, the imaginative, the logical, the
spiritual, the philosophical, the political, the everyday or any of the
other approaches that we use to make sense of life. He simply used
scientific method for solving strictly scientific questions. (Nor, actually, did Marx assert any such general priority, although Engels did.
Marx relied more on history and on philosophy, and Freud invoked
science only at times when he found it convenient.) It cannot, therefore be true that Darwin's views make theological and spiritual
explanations superfluous. He knew very well that distinct kinds of
explanation do not compete because explanations answer particular
questions.

A thing can be explained in as many different ways as there are
different kinds of question that can be asked about it and these
accounts do not clash. Thus, a political map of Europe does not
conflict with a physical one, nor a historical account of Newton's
discoveries with an analysis of their reasoning. And again, if somebody produced an account of every movement that Einstein's
neurones had made while he solved a particular problem, this story
would not have the slightest relevance to understanding his thought.
The various patterns that we see from these different angles are
not alternatives, so the different sciences by which we detect them
are not competitors. They are more like different pairs of specta-

cles used for different purposes than rival claimants contending for sovereignty.

It should be equally obvious that an evolutionary account of human origins does not displace the direct understanding that we have about human experience, but merely supplements it. It does not make the problems that afflict us about that experience unreal, so it cannot make the thought systems that we use to understand them superfluous, although it may, of course, throw new and interesting lights on them. Darwin understood this and knew that the meaning of morality was indeed a vast issue to which his own natural-historical enquiry, important though it was, would only make its own particular contribution. He read Kant, Hume, Marcus Aurelius and the rest with attention and he respected their arguments. He did not make the reductive mistake of seeing it all as quite simple.

Imperialistic reductions

Of course Le Fanu is right to complain that foolish reductive claims like this have lately been widely made. Scientism – the ambition to take over the whole of human knowledge for physics and chemistry – has indeed been flourishing. Thus Atkins:

> Scientists, with their implicit trust in reductionism, are privileged to be at the summit of knowledge, and to see further into truth than any of their contemporaries ... While poetry titillates and theology obfuscates, science liberates.
>
> (1995: 123)

> *There is no reason to believe that science cannot deal with every aspect of existence ...* (*Ibid.*: 132, emphasis added)

91

Dawkins too claims that science – apparently meaning the physical sciences – can, and some day will, answer all questions:

> Opinion among scientists, among whom I am one, will insist that, "That which we don't understand" means only, "That which we don't yet understand". Science is still working on the problem. We don't know when or even whether, we shall eventually be brought up short. (2004: 177)

This remarkable faith in an unknown future science is, however, a product of the twentieth century, not of the nineteenth. Only during the past century did increased specialization produce a scientific education so narrow that it never told its pupils that our knowledge is necessarily fragmented. They grew up with no idea that we have to use many different ways of thinking, needing different disciplines, to deal with the many aspects of the world, nor that most facts will always be beyond our understanding, however much we may extend it. Considering the way in which we seem to have evolved, our limited capacities here ought not really to surprise them, but it seems they do. Still less had they considered how our various thought patterns should be related. Unlike Einstein's generation, and even more unlike the Victorians, they simply did not see the huge, shifting and expanding conceptual background that had shaped the thought forms they rely on.

Thus their reductive enterprises, like most dramatic reductions, are really exercises in interdisciplinary politics. They are sceptical in one area in order to inflate another. Interestingly, although Atkins claims that physical science can answer all questions, he makes no suggestion about how it would actually deal with the huge mass of already recognized questions – questions historical, geographical, linguistic, mathematical, logical, psychological, philosophical and so forth, all needing their own methods – that it would face if it tried to do so. Although his vast claim shoots vaguely in the direction of the humanities its only serious target is theology – that is, religion. And religion is deposited within the scope of physical science simply by ruling that it belongs there. Thus Dawkins: "The existence of God is a scientific hypothesis like any other ... I am agnostic [about it] only to the extent that I am agnostic about fairies at the bottom of the garden" (2006: 51).

Trouble about God

This strangely casual assumption that questions arising out of people's spiritual difficulties are perfectly simple is another point on which neo-Darwinists contrast sharply with their supposed founder. Darwin did, of course, reject the rather simple Christian faith in which he had been brought up, but he never embraced simple, confident atheism either. He replied plainly to various correspondents who asked him about it, "I have never been an atheist in the sense of denying the existence of God". And, mulling over that topic in his *Autobiography*, he gave the matter serious thought:

> Another source of conviction in the existence of God, connected with the reason and not with the feelings, impresses me as having much more weight. This follows from the extreme difficulty, *or rather impossibility*, of conceiving this immense and wonderful universe, including man, ... as the result of blind chance or necessity. When thus reflecting I feel compelled to look to a First Cause having an intelligent mind in some degree analogous to that of man, and I deserve to be called a theist. (2002: 54, emphasis added)

He went on to explain the various uncertainties that then arose, especially the doubts arising from our undignified evolutionary origins. "Can the mind of man, which has, as I fully believe, been developed from a mind as low as that possessed by the lowest animal, be trusted when it draws such grand conclusions?" But this difficulty, of course, arises equally about all our thinking, including the reasonings of science. Since we do not have the thoughts of any non-evolved mind at hand to compare with our own we are in no position to assess its importance. Darwin's conclusion is that, "the mystery of the beginning of all things is insoluble and I for one must be content to remain an Agnostic" (*ibid.*).

He was not – as some people now suggest – using the term *agnostic* here as a polite euphemism for *atheist*, supplying a kindly fudge to avoid criticism and keep his wife happy. He was recognizing real mysteries and he certainly gave the word *agnostic* the literal force that he knew Huxley – who had quite recently coined it for that very purpose – had intended. It acknowledges a genuine ignorance – including ignorance about the nature of that intelligent agency – that has not, of course, been dispelled since his day either by the theory of evolution or by the discovery of the Big Bang.

The kind of position that he takes here is often called *deism*, but that name merely indicates a vast and fertile territory, not a particular doctrine. (Tom Paine, although ferociously anti-Christian, was an ardent deist and was very nearly guillotined by the French Revolutionary Convention for rejecting the compulsory atheism imposed by the Jacobins). Darwin was, in fact, well aware of how little we know, about this question or indeed about most others, which is a central point in his greatness. And that agnosticism – that continued openness to wider spiritual possibilities – is, of course, perfectly compatible with his belief in evolution, because evolution makes equally good sense either with a God or without one. Charles Kingsley surely got that point right from the Christian angle when he wrote, on reading *The Origin of Species*, "It is just as noble a conception of Deity to believe that he created primal forms capable of self-development ... as to believe that he required a fresh act of intervention to supply the *lacunas* which he himself had made" (Desmond & Moore 1991: 477).

Thus, as Kingsley and many other Christians have looked at it, if God is present, he pervades the whole process of evolution as its creator and is immanent in all of it. He is not an outside operative, a retired clockmaker or visiting engineer, dropping in to adjust the nuts and bolts. (These mechanical images, which grew up during the industrial revolution, have gravely distorted the picture). So he does not have to be invoked sporadically as a "God of the gaps" to account for points where we are especially ignorant. There should not, then, really have been a serious clash here. The only difficulty – and of course it has proved a severe one – is that it means the biblical account of creation cannot be taken literally.

That news ought not really to have shocked Christendom. As it happened, the Church Fathers, notably Augustine, had very early seen the need to treat some biblical stories as metaphors or allegories, and had often advised this. Origen pointed out that the sun and moon could not literally have been created "on the third day", because there could have been no days before they were present. This, he said, did not matter because the symbolic meaning was always the real message. Thus the Genesis story simply describes the total dependence of all creatures on a ruling benevolent spirit and does this through a myth: an imaginative vision that is the most appropriate way of bringing such vast and mystifying facts within human comprehension. The details of the story are merely shaped to make this central point clear.

Since, however, the truth of the symbolic story was so important, people naturally often did assume that biblical stories were factually true as well. Their details served to fill an enormous gap of total ignorance about the beginnings of things. In the Enlightenment, however, a quite new, sharper conception of historical accuracy developed, a critically based notion that would have astonished both the composers of Genesis and most of its earlier hearers. For the first time in human history it began to seem possible to find out what had actually happened in the remote past.

As this confidence grew, during the eighteenth century, people began to demand that the Bible should somehow be shown to be literally accurate as well as spiritually nourishing. And gradually it became clear that a choice would be needed here. Many people, however, felt that these two functions were equally sacred and made desperate efforts to bring them together somehow. This literalist campaign was strongest in the Protestant churches, where deep respect for the Bible had taken the central place that respect for the Church had held among Catholics. It was particularly strong in America because so many devout Protestants had gone there to escape disagreement at home.

This, of course, is why the discovery of the earth's antiquity by eighteenth-century geologists – long before Darwin – produced serious clashes, clashes whose political dimensions still reverberate today. These, however, are not actually conflicts between science and religion. They are disagreements within various religious communities – Christian, Muslim and Jewish – about the kind of sacredness that attaches to sacred books. Where that sacredness is held to forbid any change in traditional interpretations, the books themselves, along with these interpretations, can become objects of worship. This bibliolatry creates one more kind of reductivism, one more attempt to impose a single form of thought on a range of problems that it cannot possibly deal with. It is closely parallel to the scientistic reductions that Le Fanu rightly objects to.

5
Darwin's new broom

Which reductions do we need?

We have now looked at what Darwin actually wrote about human sociality. We have seen how far his thinking is from what his supposed disciples offer. And we have noticed how his remarks have upset people in two opposite quarters: both his self-styled followers, who think he is not reductive enough, and the various kinds of traditionalists – humanists as well as Christians – who think he is too reductive. The source of both troubles lies in his original ideas about human psychology, which differ from both these widespread positions.

One very important thing that his conception of human motivation shares with the Christian view is a realistic acceptance that conflict is central to human life: that we must always be facing new dilemmas without having ready-made answers. Where he differs from the Christian angle is in locating those conflicts *within human nature itself* – between our various naturally conflicting motives – rather than between our nature as a whole and spiritual forces for good that lie outside it. He does not see the source of evil as lying in our "animal nature" as such, while everything good comes from outside it. Instead, he sees evil as arising from the mistaken choices that we – as whole persons – make between the various elements that compose our nature. It is, as the Buddhists say, a matter of unskilful means. This is what divides his position from what St Paul writes in the Epistle to the Galatians:

> The flesh lusteth against the spirit and the spirit against the flesh and these are contrary the one to the other, so that ye cannot do the things that ye would, ... The works of the flesh are manifest, which are these – Adultery, fornication, unclean-ness, idolatry, witchcraft, hatred, variance, emulations, strife, envyings, murders [Etc] ... But the fruit of the spirit is love. joy, peace, long-suffering, gentleness, goodness, temperance [etc]. (Galatians 5:17–23)

This passage, taken on its own, does in fact suggest a simpler and more extreme view of how soul and body are related than the one that is central to Paul himself and most Christian writers. But simple and extreme views are so attractive that they easily have a disproportionate influence. This kind of entanglement between the moral life and mind–body dualism, which the Christian tradition drew from Plato, has repeatedly involved it in unrealistic forms of asceticism and has sometimes strained the consciences of Christians to breaking point. Aristotle resisted that entanglement, asserting, against Plato, the unity of the human person. He said, by contrast, that all our natural desires are desires for some real good. The fact that evil so often arises is simply due to our often being in posi-tions where desires conflict, and not understanding these dilemmas properly. In those cases what is vital is to choose the right one for the balance of the whole situation, and all the difficulties of morals concern how to do this.

A good deal of Aristotle's common sense did filter into the Christian tradition through Thomas Aquinas. But, as extreme positions are always the easiest to grasp, many Christians over the ages have absorbed the dualist drama and this has led to a great deal of unnecessary contempt and fear, both of the body itself and of the affections that were seen as belonging to it. It has also been used to justify brutality to non-human animals, which were not supposed to have souls. And in modern times, when this anti-corporeal stance might be expected to have died down, it still persists in the form of a special reverence for human intelligence, which is seen as almost supernatural, and even in an exaltation of virtual experiences over those that involve the flesh.

Darwin, of course, takes an inclusive, Aristotelian stance on these matters. As we have seen, he does not want to deny that spiritual forces may be at work behind the scenes. But he is concerned above all to insist on the presence of positive motives, social dispositions within human nature itself: motives without which the message of those higher powers could not be heard.

In understanding our actual psychological struggles, he leads us to attend to the forces within ourselves that impel us towards good as well as those that lead to evil. (Jung rather than Freud has been his successor here). He is not surprised that the conflicts occur – that our natural wishes often fit badly together – because a rough, incomplete balance of this kind between different elements is typical of the compromises produced by evolution. Here humans are simply paying the penalty – and reaping the rewards – of having moved far away from the quasi-mechanical condition of the simplest animals and become capable of choice. Our lives are more complicated than those of limpets, so we naturally have more dilemmas.

Putting natural selection in its place

With the other party, the neo-Darwinists, he does, of course, also have something in common. He does share their belief in the importance of competition as a force that has, in some sense, continually shaped our evolving nature. It has, he says, constantly determined which of two alternative tendencies shall survive. But he does not limit that competition to explicit fighting or rivalry. He includes in it everything that actually leads to survival, such as cooperation within groups. This means that, if we want to understand our predicament, we should attend to the whole range of our natural motives, good as well as bad, and to the sources of conflict between them. Simple formulae such as saying that we are naturally selfish are no substitute for doing this more difficult kind of psychology.

The neo-Darwinists have expressed their alarm at all this by ignoring the awkward parts of Darwin's writings and oversimplifying the rest under the name of Darwinism. They suppress his group selectionism as a betrayal of his one central message, which in their view was the centrality of selection working through competition between individuals. They therefore follow Huxley by inflating and dramatising this competitive process into a cosmic force. Daniel Dennett's book *Darwin's Dangerous Idea* is one long rhapsody on this theme.

Dennett explains how, as a boy, he was pleased with the idea of a universal acid, so corrosive that it can eat through anything. Fortunately he later found a theory – natural selection – that he thought could achieve this, a theory that:

> eats through every traditional concept .... Darwin's idea had been born as an answer to questions in biology, but it threatened to leak out, offering answers – welcome or not – to questions in cosmology (going in one direction) and psychology (going in the other). (1995: 63)

In psychology, Dennett uses the idea to explain all human thought, as Dawkins does, through competition among a mythical population of selfish memes, which are taken to be quasi-genes of culture. On the cosmological side he largely proceeds through an orgy of whynottery: "why couldn't that whole process itself be the product of evolution, and so forth, all the way down?" (*ibid.*), and so on, arguing that this same explanatory principle works universally.

This shows that, if you are excited enough about the drama of individual competition between humans you can project it onto any field you fancy without ever saying anything solid enough to collide with the facts. This seems also true of Atkins's view on what happened before space-time got started:

> Imagine the entities which are about to become assembled into space time as being a structureless dust ... Space Time itself emerged out of its own dust ... Think of the primordial dust as swirling momentarily into clusters. (1987: 99)

> Vast numbers of such still-born universes form [and finally the fittest one emerges]. (*Ibid.*: 103)

Thus the Big Bang itself resulted from competition between rival possibilities. Similarly, as Atkins explains, "light automatically discovers briefest paths by trying all paths and automatically eradicates all traces of its explorations, then presents itself to us as a behaviour, which we summarize as a rule" (*ibid.*: 51). Stories such as these surely raise questions about Dawkins's striking claim, made on page 1 of *The Selfish Gene*, that "we no longer have to resort to superstition when faced with the deep problems." If explanation by memes and disembodied possibilities does not constitute superstition, what does?

Darwin himself, by contrast, was so far from wanting to extend natural selection beyond the biological realm that he insisted it was not the whole explanation even within biology. He was never a crusading prophet for scientism. He never offered his evolutionary view as a wholesale substitute for current ways of understanding the human condition. He offered it as a contribution, a way of dealing with important gaps and problems in our worldview. And even within biology, he denied that natural selection was a universal explanation, remarking crossly in the sixth edition of *The Origin of Species*:

> As my conclusions have lately been much misrepresented, and it has been stated that I attribute the modification of species exclusively to natural selection, I may be permitted to remark that, in the first edition of this work, and subsequently, I placed in a most conspicuous position – namely at the close of the Introduction – the following words; "*I am convinced that natural selection has been the main, but not the exclusive, means of modification.*" This has been of no avail. Great is the power of steady misrepresentation. (6th ed. 1872: 395)

No doubt one reason why this oversimplification bothered him was that he always remained interested in Lamarck's idea of the inheritance of acquired characteristics. But that was not just a casual eccentricity. More profoundly, a destructive factor like natural selection clearly could not be the sole cause of something as complex and positive as evolutionary development. One might say, more generally, that a filter can never be the sole cause of the stuff that flows out of it. To explain that stuff you also need to understand the input. When Darwin said that thinking about the problem of the peacock's tail made him feel physically sick, he was expressing this sense of the *disproportion* between the phenomenon produced, "this immense and wonderful universe", and the proposed explanation.

He did indeed still see natural selection as the main cause of evolution. And, considering that he had just discovered it and no other plausible cause had yet been suggested this is not surprising. But he later added sexual selection and – as this passage shows – he still regarded the whole question as open. Dennett's idea of exalting natural selection into a universal causal explanation and imposing it, not just throughout biology but across all phenomena, is quite alien to Darwin. What would probably have interested him much more is the proposal, which has lately been much discussed, of examining the internal factors that fix the range of available alternatives.

Natural selection and natural creativity

It should be fairly obvious that the idea of *selection* makes no sense unless you understand that range. The notion of entirely random selection from an indefinite range – which Monod implied in his talk of casinos and lotteries, and which is often still taken for granted – is quite unrealistic. Nature is not a casino manager equalizing all chances. Natural process can only produce, at each stage, something that falls within the narrow range that lies before it, just as human selectors could not produce a bulldog from a breeding population of rabbits or oak trees. Within that range, too, all sorts of factors weight the probabilities one way or another.

In the first place, matter itself has quite definite, limited ways of shaping itself. Without any help from life or natural selection it creates surprisingly complex forms. Snow crystals develop, solar systems rotate and spiral galaxies spire; indeed, those galaxies trace out Fibonacci spirals, which are also found in the arrangement of buds and flowers on a plant. And, of course, for living things the range of possibilities is much smaller. In fact there are quite narrow limits to the ways in which it is possible to live at all, and still narrower ones to the paths available at any given point. Aerial whales or creatures on wheels may seem possible but they haven't developed. What does develop is a great inventory of surprisingly similar creatures produced by a great deal of convergence. There are numberless cases where different evolutionary lines have adopted the same solution for their problems: similar designs for an eye, a silken web or a digging organ, converging far more strongly than engineering considerations seem to require.

Jerry Fodor and Massimo Piattelli Palmarini have stated these and related points forcibly in their admirable (and only slightly mistitled) book *What Darwin Got Wrong* (2010). These authors marshal a whole spectrum of evolutionary factors other than muta-tion and selection that undermine the neo-Darwinian mantra that "slow, gradual, cumulative natural selection is the ultimate expla-nation for our existence" (Dawkins 1986: 318). They compare the neo-Darwinists' exclusive reliance on selectionism to B. F. Skinner's exclusive belief in conditioning as the sole cause of learning. As they point out, Skinner's idea became discredited because it neglected all the positive, internal factors that learning requires, factors that are needed for any actual understanding of the lessons learnt. Similarly, classical mutation and selection may indeed (they say) sometimes have an effect in evolution, but there is no reason to privilege them above a crowd of other possible causes. "Biologists have to delimit the realm of possible creatures first and only then ask about natural selection" (Fodor & Piattelli Palmerini 2010: 74).

Not only are most mutations now known to be destructive but the material of inheritance itself has turned out to be far more complex, and to provide a much wider repertoire of untapped possibilities, than used to be thought. Thus, to an impressive extent, organisms provide the materials for their own innovations. Epigenetic effects, resulting from different expressions of the same genes, can make a huge difference. And genes themselves are now known not to be independent bean-like items connected to particular transmitted traits, but aspects of a most intricate process, sensitive to all sorts of internal factors, which means that in many ways the same genes can result in a different creature. And recent work on "evo-devo" – on the evolution of paths of development – shows how these can themselves change and can change the resulting organism. Forces such as "molecular drive" that rearrange the genes can also have that effect.

Fodor and Piattelli Palmarini conclude that, since natural selection cannot possibly be the cause of all evolutionary developments:

it is vastly more plausible to suppose that the causes of these forms are to be found in the elaborate self-organizing interactions between several components that are, indeed, coded for by genes ... and the strictures dictated by physical and chemical forces ....

[It is therefore scandalous that, as] Stuart Kauffman (rightly and somewhat sadly) says, "No body of thought incorporates self-organization into the weave of evolutionary theory".

(*Ibid.*: 73–4, referring to Kauffman 1993)

The term *self-organization* here is, of course, not just a fey piece of dramatization. These are not fanciful authors who can be brushed aside as "new age". They are in fact fiercely naturalistic, secular and scientifically minded. The forces they invoke are (they insist) entirely material, but they are far more complex, far less fully understood, than has recently been assumed, so that we need to think about them in new ways. For this the theme of self-organization – the mysterious generation of patterns from within – is clearly very important. These authors see that this idea could lead to illicit anthropomorphism, yet they clearly think it better to stress the surge of activity that pervades the natural world rather than to accept the neo-Darwinian story of life as a meaningless jumble of detached atoms. As they concede, "it is very hard indeed to get an account of evolution that actually does get the *deus* out of the *machina*" (Fodor & Piattelli Palmarini 2010: 116) but they think they have found a possible way to do it.

If we respond by asking them for an all-purpose theory – for some other single evolutionary mechanism corresponding to Dennett's universal acid – they reply that none is needed.

> We don't know what the mechanism of evolution is. As far as we can make out, nobody knows exactly how phenotypes evolve. We think that, quite possibly, they evolve in lots of different ways; perhaps there are as many distinct kinds of causal routes to the fixation of phenotypes as there are different kinds of natural histories of the creatures whose phenotypes they are. (*Ibid.*: 153)

Each case, they think, must be investigated on its own merits and in its own terms. Thus they entirely reject adaptationism: the view that evolution always – or even usually – selects for adaptive traits. In their view this whole metaphor of *selection* implies an illicit reference to intention, to the hidden purpose of some selecting mind. This is where they differ from Conway Morris, who – as we shall see – is quite prepared to take on that implication.

On another central point, however, Fodor and Piattelli Palmarini are in agreement with him. In a chapter interestingly called "The Return of the Laws of Form", they note the importance of naturally occurring patterns such as the Fibonacci spirals just mentioned, and mention the work of earlier theorists such as D'Arcy Thompson who studied the role of such patterns in the shaping of organisms. Thompson's work, which appeared in 1917, was for some time neglected because it did not fit the selectionist temper of the times. More lately, however, not only has neo-Darwinism stopped looking so convincing but general questions of this kind about the origins of form have been very interestingly discussed, for instance by Ilya Prigogine and Isabelle Stengers in *Order Out Of Chaos* (1984).

The force of this idea first really came home to me when I went sailing in the Hebrides soon after reading *Order Out of Chaos*. In those seas, great cliffs repeatedly rose up before us that seemed to be coated in organ pipes, stands of huge hexagonal basalt pillars that were shaped, apparently, by the colossal lava flows that first formed Scotland. Those flows also created Fingal's Cave and indeed the Giant's Causeway, where tourists constantly tread on an uneven pavement of neat hexagons, snapped off at regular breaking-points and set together so closely that you can only just get a knife between them.

This kind of structured creativity in matter, which is something that was originally noted by Goethe, will surely prove central to the enquiry Fodor and Piattelli Palmarini are calling for. Conway Morris too is convinced of its importance:

> Life depends both on a suitable chemistry, whose origins are literally cosmic, and on the realities of evolutionary adaptation. The chemistry is acknowledged but largely ignored; the adaptation is often derided as a wishful fantasy .... Life shows a kind of homing instinct .... Despite its fecundity and baroque richness, life is also strongly constrained. The net result is a genuine creation, almost unimaginably rich and beautiful, but one also with an underlying structure in which, given enough time, the inevitable must happen. (2003: 20)

If, by contrast, evolution had really been a casino the resulting world would have been a meaningless mix-up, not this widespread order that so deeply impressed Darwin and that still impresses us. Conway Morris notes the strange way in which this persistent order has been neglected in recent biology:

Rerun the tape of history, so S. J. Gould would have us believe, and the end result will be an utterly different biosphere. Most notably there will be nothing like a human ... Yet what we know of evolution suggests the exact reverse; convergence is ubiquitous and the constraints of life make the various biological properties very probable, if not inevitable ....

(*Ibid.*: 283)

It is, he says, far more natural and rational to read the universe that science now shows us as being in some sense a purposive whole than deliberately to ignore all this evidence for system, evidence that is actually what leads people to study science in the first place. Human conscious purposiveness then appears, not as a bizarre exception in a jumbled world, but as just one form of a more general property, a directionality that is immanent and widespread throughout the cosmos.

The strange survival of purposive thinking

Scientifically minded people have, of course, recently avoided any such thoughts for fear of seeming to invoke a creative God. They have claimed, indeed, that they no longer need to use teleology, that is, the Aristotelian method of explaining phenomena by function and aim. In fact, however, the language of function and aim is still used throughout biology exactly as it always was and as it obviously needs to be, protected only by an occasional explanation that it is really only a manner of speaking – a metaphor. Things, it seems, happen "as if" for a purpose.

Metaphors, however, are always brought in for a reason, and a thought form as widely used as this would hardly have persisted if it was not really needed. It is interesting that this teleological language is particularly rampant in the neo-Darwinian disciplines of socio-biology and evolutionary psychology, studies that have always been especially hostile to the idea of creative gods. Immense efforts are put here into finding an "evolutionary function" for everything from homosexuality to nose-picking and the unbridled dynastic ambitions of genes add the necessary drama to these discussions by supplying the guiding purpose of all development.

Genes, however, can probably not be used much longer in this role because, as we have seen, it is emerging that they do not play anything like as central a part in development as was once supposed. And, what is more important, no one else need be nominated to fill that central role either. Questions about who, if anybody, owns the purposes that animate the living world need not arise at all when we are doing biology, however important they may be at other times. Nor can it be useful to suggest – as some have done – that there is a mysterious entity called Natural Selection, or indeed Chance, whose business it is to decide where we are all going.

Aristotle himself did not invoke a creator god or any other agent in his biological enquiries. He simply asked systematically, as his successors have done, what various things in the living world are *for*. We can usually find plenty of plausible suggestions about this because our own experience, and that of the creatures round us, gives us well-grounded general ideas about possible aims – aims such as health, happiness, prosperity and long life – which are perfectly adequate at the biological level. The interesting question is then: what values go with these aims? When we think about the health of an oak wood or a gull colony, are we assuming that health is good or desirable? If so, ought we somehow to disinfect our thoughts and destroy that assumption? Does objectivity require that all such judgments should be value free?

This kind of suggestion has worried scientifically minded people quite a lot. It is an extension of the perfectly reasonable point that we should not project features onto gulls or oak trees that are actually peculiar to humans. But it extends this idea so far that it destroys the concept of health altogether, making the whole idea unusable. *Health* simply means a good and proper physical state for an organism; a state that appears to be its aim. It is a term, like *importance* or *danger*, which explicitly links certain facts with their appropriate values on the basis of other facts in the world. To say that this gull colony is *less healthy* than it used to be is to note both a real fact about the world and the kind of harm that this fact is doing: the purposes that it frustrates. And, if we ask whether the purposes are themselves objective, we can see that the gulls do actually have purposes to which this decline of the colony is contrary, and so do the people who are concerned about them.

More generally, it is an objective fact that all living things behave purposively: that is, they all strive and struggle to live in the way that their particular nature requires. They do not, of course, need to be conscious to do this. An acorn that is buried under a paving stone will go to enormous lengths to grow past or round the stone or, if necessary, to lift it up in its struggles, because this is the action necessary for a proper oak seed. An enquirer who did not understand this purposive striving would have no chance at all of understanding what the acorn was doing. That is why it is not actually realistic to suggest, as Dawkins does, in the passage mentioned earlier, that realism calls on us to think of the universe as devoid of purpose:

The universe we observe has precisely the properties we should expect if there is at bottom no design, no purpose, no evil and no good, nothing but blind, pitiless indifference. As that unhappy poet A. E. Housman put it:

For Nature, heartless, witless Nature
Will neither care nor know.

DNA neither cares nor knows. DNA just is. And we dance to
its tune.   (Dawkins 1995: 155)

But this universe actually contains many things like acorns that
unmistakeably do have purposes: living, striving things that strive
because for them – as for us – some conditions really are good,
others really evil. It therefore contains a great deal of design. And it
is remarkable what strong teleological language Dawkins uses here,
even in describing disorganization. Thus DNA suddenly appears
as an active anti-God figure in charge of the non-caring business,
a powerful agent that, because of its "blind, pitiless indifference",
actively forces us to dance to its tune. How would you do that
without a purpose?

Meaning and meaninglessness

Dawkins's universe, then, is not actually a meaningless one; it has
a positive, sinister meaning. Atkins is equally colourful, declaring
that, "Every action is corruption and every restoration contributes
to degradation" (1987: 35); "Even free-will is ultimately corruption" (*ibid.*: 39). Weinberg, too, before complaining that the world
is pointless, also says that this is "an unimaginably hostile universe".
Perhaps he means only that we could not survive in outer space.
But, considering that this is the universe that has given us all that
we have, his lurid description seems rather peculiar.

A. E. Housman, when he wrote of "heartless, witless Nature", was
not telling any such cosmic story. He was merely lamenting that the
landscape he loved could not be expected to love him back again. This
proper and human kind of regret gives no ground for claiming that
science tells us to deny the presence of purpose in a world where in
fact we observe purpose all the time, still less to credit chemicals such

as DNA with having manipulative purposes. It is plain that we would not be able to understand the living world around us at all if we did not think of many things in it as purposive – or, of course, if we were so lacking in purpose ourselves that we did not follow our thoughts through to their conclusion. And we certainly could not do science.

Interest in purpose has, however, obviously led people in many cultures, including out own, to religious thinking and often to ideas about God or gods that are of great importance in their lives. The idea that science should have nothing to do with these themes has been strong in recent times but, as Conway Morris points out, it is not particularly scientific. The phenomenon is real, so there is nothing superstitious about enquiring into it:

> So, at some point and somehow, given that evolution has produced sentient species with a sense of purpose, it is reasonable to take the claims of theology seriously. In recent years there has been a resurgence of interest in the connections that might serve to reunify the scientific world-view with the religious instinct. Much of the discussion is tentative, and the difficulties in finding an accommodation remain daunting, but it is more than worth the effort. In my opinion it will be our lifeline. (2003: 328)

This return to the central interests of the founders of modern science – devout men such as Newton, Bacon and Boyle – may well sound odd to many of today's academics, who are often as sure as Boyle and Newton were that their views on religion are scientifically grounded. But other scientists take a similar line. Thus the cosmologist Paul Davies, after considering the remarkable physical coincidences that have lately been noticed in the cosmos – the precise adjustments of natural forces that suggest the presence of fine tuning designed to make life possible – remarks:

It seems to me that there is a genuine scheme of things; the universe is "about" something. But I am equally uneasy about dropping the whole set of problems in the lap of an arbitrary God, or abandoning all further thought and declaring existence ultimately to be a mystery ....

Even though I do not believe Homo Sapiens to be more than an accidental by-product of natural processes ... I do believe that *life and mind are etched deeply into the fabric of the universe*, perhaps through a shadowy, half-glimpsed life-principle.   (2006: 302–3, emphasis added)

Theorists who are determined to resist any such teleological approach tend now to dismiss this human readiness to see purpose as a mere quirk of evolution – an unfortunate eccentricity of our species, probably acquired because it had the evolutionary function of cheering our ancestors up. But the mere fact that a belief cheers us up, or even that it could have helped with survival, does not show that that belief is groundless. An alternative possibility is always that it just happens to be true. This, presumably, is what we think about our – equally unproved and equally instinctive – belief in the regularity of nature, which (of course) is a necessary presupposition for science.

Another interesting parallel case here is our universal belief that the people around us are not robots: that they are sensitive creatures with feelings like our own, that their feelings affect their actions and that we often know what those feelings are. Hard-nosed behaviourists and epiphenomenalists, who officially reject some or all of this, can, if they wish, dismiss these claims to empathy as merely soothing mechanisms supplied by evolution because they have eased social intercourse. They can point out, too, that the reality of other people's feelings has not been scientifically proved. Most of us, however, would probably see that scepticism as misdirected.

This belief in a plurality of thinking subjects, which grounds our concept of objectivity, is so essential for our worldview that our own thinking literally could not go on without it. We well know that we must be critical about how we use it: that it can sometimes make us impute consciousness wrongly, as when we personify cars. But these borderline mistakes can be corrected. They don't require us to abandon so central and necessary a presupposition.

I suspect that the very general concept of purpose at work in the world has a similar standing. The way in which, when thrown out through the door, it keeps coming straight back through the window, and particularly the way in which it has contrived to dominate the concept of evolution today, surely suggests this. And – as we saw when discussing Darwin's views on the matter – the mere fact that our minds have been produced by evolution does not undermine it. That history affects all our thinking equally.

Social atomism and economics

These are, of course, vast metaphysical topics, which might seem remote from the topic of this book. The neo-Darwinists, however, have invoked them by their vast claim that natural selection is the guiding explanatory principle for all thought, a claim which is certainly metaphysical and which they treat as central to Darwin's message. Against this notion, I am suggesting that the idea of natural selection has actually few uses outside biology and that even there – as was already clear to Darwin – it cannot possibly be the sole explanation of development. It only makes sense against a background of knowledge about the alternatives available: both detailed knowledge about physical tendencies and a much wider conception of how the whole cosmos works. And to this natural selection makes no useful contribution.

The reason why this expanded idea of natural selection has attracted people is surely not this illusory usefulness in explanation. It is its dramatic appeal in an age obsessed by individual competition. Just as Herbert Spencer delighted Americans in the 1880s by hailing the millionaire bandits of capitalism as the advance-guard of evolution, so the title of *The Selfish Gene* delighted people who were tired of the enforced sacrifices imposed by war and were pleased to think that self-indulgence was now what evolution demanded.

Of course, the book itself did provide some real knowledge about evolution. But it had a much deeper effect in shaping, through its rhetoric, contemporary forms of the social atomism that is our central topic. Today, as in the nineteenth century, individualist propaganda is phrased in economic terms drawn from the spectacular financial gyrations of the time. The fantastic idea of the "bottom line" – money as the final arbiter of reality – grew up then and is prevalent again today.

This is particularly clear in the language now chosen to describe the workings of evolution. The talk is all of financial competition jazzed up by military images: rival investments, suckers and grudgers, hawk and dove strategies, war games and the like. These metaphors can, of course, quite reasonably be used to bring out particular points. But they are only one set out of dozens that might just as well be used to bring out something different. The cumulative effect of concentrating on them is to dramatize evolution in a most misleading way. As Brian Goodwin points out:

> Competition ... is often described as the driving force of evolution, pushing organisms willy-nilly up the fitness landscape if they are going to survive in the struggle with their neighbours ... However, there is as much co-operation in biology as there is competition. Mutualism and symbiosis – organisms living together in states of mutual dependency such as lichens

that combine a fungus with an alga in happy harmony, or the bacteria in our guts, from which we benefit as well as they – are an equally universal feature of the biological realm. Why not argue that "co-operation" is the great source of innovation in evolution, as in the enormous step, aeons ago, of producing a eukaryotic cell ... by the co-operative union of two or three prokaryotes? (1994: 166)

Why not indeed? The reason why this would sound odd today is not, I think, that individual competition is a scientifically central concept but that social atomism is the prevailing myth of the time. To see how this has come about, it will be worth while to look back a little further at the history of individualism.

6
The self's strange adventures

Who are we?

How, then, did modern individualism arise? No doubt, if Thomas Hobbes had not lived, someone else would have set it off and would be hailed as its founder. The kind of communal, hierarchical thinking that we now call feudal was becoming unworkable, so someone else would have attacked it. But since Hobbes, with his deep ardour and amazing turns of phrase, was actually present, he has become known as its spokesman. And although much of what he wrote is far more subtle than his later reputation would suggest, his influence on European thought has been so strong that it is now reasonable to say that Hobbes invented the modern ego – the ego that thinks it exists quite on its own.

We shall concentrate here, then, on his extreme statements, the mantras that have caught on and are still affecting our lives, without trying to do justice to his subtleties. Central to these mantras was surely his cry, in *Leviathan*, that the natural state of human life was one of ceaseless "war of all against all". Human beings, he said, were naturally pure, relentless egoists who could only be brought to live in harmony by fear of the threatening power of government. "Of the voluntary acts of every man the Object is some good to himself". Without government, therefore, their life would be just a zero-sum game: "solitary, poor, nasty, brutish and short" (pt I, ch. 13).

This was not mere rhetoric. Hobbes was responding to an ongoing series of civil wars that were nominally wars of religion. He couldn't stand people being conned by pious nonsense into fighting battles that didn't concern them, and ending up dead. He therefore proposed a new principle of political obligation, designed to stop humans killing each other for trivial reasons. The state does not, said Hobbes, have a sweeping authority based on the divine right of kings. The state exists only as a means of self-preservation for its citizens. What justifies its authority is, he said, simply the social contract, a tacit agreement by all members to obey government in return for the protection of their own lives. They are only required to obey it in so far as it gives them that protection.

This may well sound pretty convincing. Its more awkward side is Hobbes's idea that, to make the contract work, each individual citizen must be considered as wholly separate, a unit entirely devoted to its own safety. Any outside obligation, whether to God or to other people, would weaken the self-preservative motive on which the contract depends. God therefore vanished entirely and Hobbes went to drastic lengths to shoot down all possible human social claims, reducing them to enlightened self-interest. All our passions, he said, may be "reduced to the desire for Power" (pt I, ch. 8): essentially, the power to protect ourselves. Thus all morality – not just its political aspect but the whole of it – is valid only so far as it serves that ruling purpose.

If, for instance, you ask about virtue, he tells you, "Force and Fraud are in War the two cardinal Virtues". Honour, he says, "consisteth only in Opinion of Power" (pt I, ch. 13). More alarmingly still, he rules that "the Value or Worth of a man is, as of all other things, his Price, namely as much as would be given for the Use of his Power" (pt

I, ch. 10). That is, the man himself has no value; his worth depends entirely on how much we need him at the time. If that need ceases he may become worthless tomorrow. Moreover, if we ask about any apparently outgoing feelings we may have, such as compassion for other people's sufferings – feelings that might seem to give us a duty to those people – we are told that these feelings themselves are just indirect forms of self-interest. "Grief for the Calamity of another is Pity, and ariseth from the Imagination that the like Calamity may befall himself" (pt I, ch. 10).

This is a particular form of reductivism that moralists use when they want to shock people into honestly admitting their less respectable motives. They do it by pointing out how essential those motives are to our lives. Epicurus, Nietzsche and Freud have similarly claimed to reduce human psychology to a single dominant motive – pleasure, power or sex – and the exaggeration often wakes people up, showing them their own confusions. Hobbes shared this ambition to make people more realistic. He attacked current euphemisms so as to force people to admit certain nasty truths about themselves: so as to make them stop their foolish, wasteful activities. This is good, but true realism demands a bit more than this. It asks for more attention to the complexity of the facts. It does not actually mix well with propaganda.

Like those other theorists, Hobbes did indeed make people aware of some important psychological facts. Since his time, the thought that each individual's interest must be considered because, for each of us, our own safety is so terribly important, has been built into the political vision of the Enlightenment. It lies at the root of modern individualism. But – also like those others – he did it at the cost of bringing in his own distortions. The picture that he finally displays is not straight fact. It is one more romantic reforming vision: a dream of strange, isolated, clear-headed beings who are both far more self-absorbed and enormously better at rational planning than any actual members of our species.

Is egoism a psychological fact?

Right from the start, his critics have therefore asked: do you mean that we actually *are* like this – that we are beings with no natural sociable feelings (which doesn't seem very plausible) – or that we ought to be so (which is even less convincing)? This question is awkward because Hobbes probably wanted to say part of both these things, but he put them both in such extreme forms that it gets very hard to combine them.

In a way, his central point was probably the moral one: that we *ought* not to risk our own and other people's lives and interests in the outrageously thoughtless ways that we often do. Hobbes was strongly opposed to dumb wars. And he thought that the only way to avoid these wars was to be *rational* in the very odd sense that economists have since developed, that is, to become economic men, wholly devoted to our own interests.

Clearly there is much in this. If everybody were thoroughly devoted to ensuring their own safety and free from silly ambitions, most of the harm that is done in the world would never happen. But does it follow that we ought to run our lives like this if we don't happen to want to?

Hobbes was naturally not going to give the accepted answer here by talking about God. He replied that actually this is what we *really* want already, and we would know that now if we were a bit more clear-headed. This is a factual psychological claim, one that is convincing up to a point, but rather hard to reconcile with many of the ways in which quite clear-headed people often do behave, such as riding motorbikes and climbing mountains, let alone committing suicide or devoting much of their lives to others.

Can we somehow sort out this dilemma? That would surely be the right way to ride the Leviathan – to profit by Hobbes's strange but penetrating political message without being landed with an unrealistic psychology that is liable to complicate our lives.

Freedom and desolation

Hobbes has left us with a fascinating dilemma. Politically, his description of humans as wholly self-interested beings, only linked by a social contract, has been most helpful. It has shaped the idea of freedom that lies behind modern individualism. Repeatedly, it has allowed reformers to widen their constituencies; to spread the franchise; to insist that there is no substitute for "one man – or even one woman – one vote".

On the other hand, in personal life it is not half so helpful. The trouble there is that not all our relations with the people round us are power relations. Although we do very often want to be free from their demands, we also badly want to be free to make demands on them, and all these demands form parts of patterns that, as a whole, we may still want to be involved in. If you play the violin you need orchestras; if you like to argue, you need an opponent. However tiresome other people are, we do not really want to get rid of them.

When we worry about this, it surely emerges that freedom, as an ideal, is merely a blank form, negative and neutral, a name for getting rid of something or other. Its meaning is only clear when we specify just what we want to be free *from* and free *for*. Fanny Trollope, for instance, noted an interesting use of it when she heard an American acquaintance asking, "What's the use of coming to a free country if you can't do what you want with your own born slaves?" Such arguments serve to express a particular choice that has been made between various possible kinds of freedom. And we do constantly need to make such choices. Some demands, after all, may be constitutive parts of our lives: things without which we would not be ourselves.

For instance, what about families? Freedom from them – especially freedom of children from their elders – has been a prime theme of individualistic thinking from the eighteenth-century novelists on to R. D. Laing. And the little that Hobbes says on the topic shows just why it mattered so much. Families have indeed constantly been treated as power structures, centres of government. In a state of nature, says Hobbes, families arise merely because "a man maketh his children submit themselves, and their children, to his government, as being able to destroy them if they refuse" (*Leviathan*, pt I, ch. 17). Unless there is some wider social contract, a family is, he says, simply "a little Monarchy, whether that Family consist of a man and his children, or of a man and his servants, or of a man and his children and servants together" (pt I, ch. 20).

We may notice something odd about this list of possibilities and we will come back to it in a moment. The main idea, however, is that accepting the sovereign as protector gives him total authority over the subjects. Unlike some more user-friendly contract theorists, Hobbes does not base this claim on the subjects' having actually chosen the sovereign. His point is simply that they contract together to accept government of some kind rather than civil war. Their need for safety is so desperate that they must just obey the sovereign that they happen to have at the time.

He treats any suggestion of less drastic motives for compliance – which might seem particularly appropriate in the family case – with great contempt. Gratitude, for instance, is, he says, only disguised resentment. "To have received from one, to whom we think ourselves equal, greater benefits than there is hope to requite, disposeth to counterfeit Love, but really secret Hatred". And pity, which might also sometimes seem relevant, is, as he has told us, only "Grief for the Calamity of another, [which] ariseth from the imagination that the like Calamity may befall himself" (pt I, ch. 6).

Here, as we have seen, Hobbes deliberately uses brutal language as part of his campaign to break through humbug by horrifying people. Like Nietzsche and other reductive prophets, he wants to drive home unmentionable truths to us. And to some extent this fierce rhetoric does work. It forces us to see real and odious facts about our emotional constitution, facts that we need to accommodate somehow in any honest worldview. These prophets, however, do not help us much in our attempts to make this accommodation. Their stories are so one-sided that we know they can only be giving us one side of the truth. Moreover, since there are many such one-sided stories, we need different philosophers, and a different approach if we are to fit them into the world.

More dilemmas

Another difficulty is that Hobbes leaves it rather uncertain what people should do when they are not sure what course will actually best preserve them. When *Leviathan* first came out, its doctrine delighted the Royalists by seeming to call for loyalty to the king. But, once the king was defeated and Cromwell was made Protector, they began to see its drawbacks and Hobbes became very unpopular with them. His doctrine – which is essentially that you mustn't revolt unless you can – conflicts with the kinds of principle and party loyalty that usually guide people at a political level. Yet it does represent a common-sense pragmatism, which also plays an important part there.

His suggestion that this principle also obtains within the family obviously raises these difficulties, and many others too. Certainly there are power struggles there. Sons do revolt against fathers. But trying to resolve these problems simply in terms of power usually works so badly that the suggestion of justifying traditional ideas of paternal authority in this way is most unhelpful. Hobbes's proposing it shows just how powerful and entrenched those traditional ideas still were. That is why Romantic literature is full of stories of young people struggling, often successfully, to escape from the prisons built by their uncomprehending parents and parent figures.

Often, however, their first act after escaping is to enchain themselves again by getting married. And here at last we encounter that awkward female family member whom Hobbes forgot when he made his list of possibilities. I think the reason why he and his fellow theorists found it so hard to see this person is that they really did not think of her as a substantial social item at all. They saw her as padding, put there to ease the collisions between the solid, rational objects who had signed the contract. After a time, however, issues about her point of view and her relations to those around her inevitably did begin to surface. And at that point marriage itself began to come into question. Mightn't it too become a prison?

Reformers such as Mary Shelley and the Mills thought that it might. They campaigned vigorously to loosen its bars, hoping that, in the end, it might come to be seen as unnecessary and could be abandoned. This is a simple issue, they said. Either you love each other or you do not. So you straightforwardly decide either to live together or to part, making, of course, responsible arrangements for the children, if you have any. But might it perhaps be wiser not to have them in the first place? Then you are really free to do as you choose ...

All this later became part of a much wider campaign, conducted by thinkers such as Nietzsche and the existentialists, to exalt freedom above all other ideals, isolating modern individuals in pure and heroic independence. Like all such one-sided advice, this campaign ignores crucial aspects of our nature. It assumes that we are independent items, isolated brains, intelligent billiard balls that need no sustenance and could choose to live anywhere. But we are actually earthly organisms, framed to interact continually with the complex ecosystems of which we are a tiny part. For us, *bonds* are not just awkward restraints. They are lifelines. Although we all need some solitude and some independence, total isolation is for us a desolate and meaningless state. In fact it is about the worst thing that can happen to us.

We really need to become clearer about this because the image that we have of our own nature has a deep effect on how we live. Most humans, throughout most of history, have surely seen themselves as parts of a greater whole, continuous both with the life around them and with whatever higher powers may be acting within it. They have not aimed to become independent of it, much less (as is now sometimes suggested) to run the whole universe.

Campaigners for extreme individualism have depicted this whole tradition of acceptance as something childish, an unsophisticated stage that we merely pass through on our way to becoming fully adult individuals. I am suggesting that, to the contrary, this extreme individualism is itself just a local and limited point of view, like other cultural world-pictures. It is part of an imagery that has been quite useful for political purposes but cannot serve as a general view of life. It is one of the many partial visions that we must use in our attempt to forge a workable worldview. There is nothing specially grown-up about treating it as a final revelation.

Which way is left?

Individualism puzzles us today because it is not one cause but many. Since individuals have many-sided natures, they have all kinds of different needs, which can conflict. Although from outside a person's interests may seem obvious, questions often arise about which aspect of the self is to prevail, and which dangers it should specially fear. Sometimes we seem to have many selves and are not sure which of them should take charge.

Hobbes's approach had the great advantage of answering these questions clearly. His drastic metaphor of War concentrates attention wholly on survival, which is simple because it affects the whole person. And the means he chose for survival were also simple; namely cooperation and civic obedience.

Of course this suggestion caught on widely and still has great force, especially in times of disorder. The trouble about it is that although people do value survival, they have other interests too – other aspects of their natures – which often outweigh even the wish to survive. Prominent among these is the wish for freedom. And freedom, as we have seen, comes in many shapes, calling for all sorts of possibilities.

Hobbes, writing in a time of extreme disorder, thought that these various demands must simply be brushed aside. He saw no alternative to invoking an absolute ruler. Since his time, however, absolute rulers have been tried and have not turned out too well, even as guardians of survival. People have therefore developed other forms of government that are designed not just to keep people alive, but also to give them more choice about how to live.

This is the point at which the immense complexity of human motivation comes into play. Democracies try to find a workable way of life by balancing the various emphases that the different sides of our characters call for. And one constant cause of friction here is disagreement about how much we want our governments to control us in the first place. About this the political drive of the Enlightenment splits into two factions, one more devoted to order, the other to freedom – one pointing towards socialism, the other towards anarchy. Usually they are both counted as parts of the Left, because both opposed the Royalists who sat on the right in the French Revolutionary Assembly. But during the past century they have existed in fierce opposition. Their respective patron saints are, of course, Marx and Nietzsche.

Randian individuals

Both these strands still incorporate many of Hobbes's original ideas, although they sometimes use them in ways that would greatly have surprised Hobbes. For instance Ayn Rand, the American prophetess who preached extreme individualism as the gospel of laissez-faire capitalism in the mid twentieth century, ardently shared Hobbes's belief in a war of all against all, a contest that is entirely about power. But the message that she drew from it was exactly opposite to his. Hobbes, who concentrated on literal warfare, had chiefly been struck by the thought that wars can kill you. So he stressed the need to control them by supporting the social contract.

Rand, by contrast, reacted to the idea of a universal war by saying "OK, then, let's win it". She countered Hobbes's overconfidence in despotic government with an even greater confidence in the modern American myth of the heroic individual. Her theme is the rugged excellence of "men of the mind" – certain grand individuals such as tycoons and inventors – and the need to prevent the state from ever interfering with them by regulation. Clearly identifying herself, and her readers, with these people, she writes that they should never be expected to consider the rest of the populace, who are "parasites" and "mindless hordes". She denounces all altruism as evil. "The man who speaks to you of sacrifice is speaking of slaves and masters, and intends to be the master". Here, alongside Hobbes, we hear echoes of Nietzsche's denunciations of slave morality and we shall come back to this in a moment.

Rand's writings are extreme, yet they have had great influence because she was simply carrying to their logical conclusion ideas that were already extremely powerful in the United States. Alan Greenspan was, it seems, her ardent disciple, as was Ronald Reagan. A survey in 1991 declared her book *Atlas Shrugged* "the most influential book on American lives after the Bible". And more recently financial alarms have again shot her books to the top of the best-seller list. Her extreme horror of government probably springs partly from her having been brought up in the USSR. But, more widely, it also clearly feeds on the kind of paranoiac resentment against any kind of authority by which unlucky people often relieve their feelings, rather than looking for effective ways of political action. Noam Chomsky has called her deeply evil. This may seem like taking her too seriously, but we surely do need to take seriously the ideas that she stands for.

It is interesting that we see here two prophets of individualism recommending such wholly opposite paths. Politically, as I have suggested, they represent the two ends of the Enlightenment spectrum: the totalitarian end and the anarchistic one. Rand, however, adds to the anarchistic end something peculiarly American: an apparently infinite faith in the market's power to produce good out of disorder. Today, as market mechanisms explode all around us, this doctrine may lose some of its appeal. Yet it is deeply rooted and may prove hard to shift. It is not clear whether Rand's many readers have noticed this change in the world or whether they still simply take her books to show that the government is always wrong.

What is war?

What chiefly emerges here is surely how important it is, when we are confronted with these extreme and simple doctrines, to understand the guiding visions behind them and, in particular, just what danger they aim to protect us against. The motive to which Rand centrally appeals is the horror of being ordered about, a horror whose forms range from perfectly rational objection to bad government to what used to be called infantile omnipotence – the childish hope of total control. This kind of fear, intelligently disciplined, is indeed an important part of our emphasis on liberty, but it is not intelligent to erect it on its own into a heroic stance of self-admiration.

Hobbes too touches a deep and legitimate chord in invoking our fear of death and destruction. Both these themes have a real and serious place in our lives. But neither of them can possibly rule us altogether, as both these prophets want it to. And the assumption of a war of all against all that underlies both of them is less clear than it looks. If we do not find either of their prescriptions for dealing with it convincing it is worth while looking for what may be wrong with the assumption itself.

We are so used to the phrase "war of all against all" that we scarcely notice its oddity. But it is actually very odd, because the word *war* denotes something exceptional, a kind of emergency. When politicians now claim to be "at war" during what is actually peacetime, they do it to excuse actions that would normally be thought wrong. This, they are saying, is a crisis in which normal standards are suspended. But that claim only makes sense against a background where those standards do apply, a normal life that gives meaning to the exception.

Obviously, too, talking of war contrasts our enemies sharply with our friends and allies, towards whom we now feel unusual warmth. As Darwin rightly remarked, "it is no argument against savage man being a social animal that the tribes inhabiting adjacent districts are almost always at war with each other, for the social instincts never extend to all the individuals of the same species" (85). Although his "almost always" is an exaggeration, Darwin is plainly right here. Humans resemble other social animals in that their hostility to outsiders is the flipside of strong friendliness towards their own group. The distinction between friends and enemies is as central to human life as it is to the lives of wolves, meerkats and chimpanzees. Yet Hobbes's formula treats both these distinctions as mere invented, artificial devices. In a state of nature, he says, there is equal and unchanging hostility to all. The selective, cooperative friendliness that we normally see is just an institution, a safety measure devised by our intellects, something comparable to the rule of the road.

Other early theorists as well as Hobbes often gave this strictly intellectual explanation of human sociability. Assuming that people had once been solitary, they asked: how, then, did they ever get together? They too thought this must have been due to intelligent planning, assuming that, as somebody once put it, language had been invented by a congress of hitherto speechless elders who had agreed to assemble and determine the rules of grammar. But this does not sound very plausible.

If, however, you look at the issue zoologically instead, as Darwin did, these difficulties vanish. It becomes clear that the human species did not arise as an isolated miracle but as just one in a wide spectrum of other social creatures. The inborn sociability that these creatures all share actually provides the only possible context in which language could ever have developed. Speech only makes sense as a device for creatures who were already intensely sociable, creatures interested in each other who already communicated eagerly, but who needed to do it better. And, suitably enough, our immediate neighbours on that spectrum are indeed the great apes, who, like other primates, are well known for their rich variety of social interaction. It would have been an extraordinary evolutionary step if, in this situation, our species had reverted to the simpler, ego-bound emotional constitution that suits a crocodile.

This, however, has important consequences. It means that the intellect of which we are so proud is not really our prime mover. It is not the inventor of our social nature. Instead, it is a later, benign outgrowth and instrument of that nature. Before we are thinkers, we are lovers and haters, creatures deeply aware of those around us and fully integrated into their life. As soon as we start to think, our thoughts draw their force from those rich flows of natural feeling.

Our intellect enriches them further by helping to shape them, not by despotically ruling them.

Early Enlightenment thinkers, however, were so shocked by the confusions of their age that they thought reason must be put in sole charge to clear up the mess on the simplest possible set of premises. They therefore produced a set of dazzlingly simple philosophical maps that still influence us today – striking world-pictures, or rather world-diagrams, each of which centres on some serious truth, but stresses it so one-sidedly as to end up by distorting it. And, as individualism has developed, Hobbes's egoistic psychological diagram has been among the most influential of these.

Those sages cannot, of course, be blamed for failing to see the evolutionary considerations that, as I have just suggested, radically undermine Hobbes's account of human motivation. They did not know about these things. But today we do. It does seem really strange that Darwin's speculations in *The Descent of Man*, exploring ways in which we can try to understand our social nature, should have been so widely ignored, even by those who claim to follow him.

The journey inwards, 1: Mill

This neglect is, as I am suggesting, just one aspect of the Enlightenment's intense commitment to the individualistic side of the dialectic that always goes on between private and public interests. Politically, that commitment has increasingly built up institutions in the West that are designed to give each citizen his or her own voice, and they do indeed sometimes manage to do this. With that in mind, reformers have rejected and abandoned Hobbes's preference for despotic rulers. Instead, they have increasingly tried to organize government by consent, while still keeping things peaceful enough to make people feel that their lives are safe.

Does this project count as *individualistic*? It is so in the sense that it aims to do equal justice to everyone. But of course, in large and complex societies, it involves very elaborate arrangements that actually limit people's personal choices in all kinds of ways. We have to obey the majority. Institutions designed to protect our lives – which Hobbes saw as everyone's prime aim – chronically limit freedom. In fact the first two ideals of the French Revolution – liberty and equality – are in chronic conflict. And as people gradually begin to feel that their lives are secure, they increasingly resent these restraints. It turns out that each person's aim is not only to stay alive but to find his own kind of fulfilment while doing so.

That fulfilment, too, often involves the other communal achievements that count as part of human progress: art, science, technology. But these activities too are only made possible by sacrifices of liberty. Societies that get more civilized inevitably get more organized, curtailing everybody's freedom. This increasingly riles them. Nabokov celebrated, at the end of *Lolita*, the wonderful release felt by a driver who had simply decided to drive on the wrong side of the road. That release did not indeed last for long, but he thought it entirely worth while.

This reaction against restraint has naturally been very widespread, even if it is usually less dramatically expressed. Ever since the Romantic revival the emphasis has moved away from individual survival to individual freedom and to explaining the ideals that make that freedom important. In his book *On Liberty*, John Mill made the point using forceful machine imagery, which has become still more relevant since his day. He wrote:

> It really is of importance, not only what men do but what manner of men they are that do it ... Supposing it were possible to get houses built, corn grown, battles fought, causes tried, and even churches erected and prayers said, *by machinery* – by

automatons in human form – it would be a considerable loss to exchange for these automatons even the men and women who at present inhabit the more civilised parts of the world, and who assuredly are but starved specimens of what nature can and will produce. Human nature is not a machine to be built after a model, and set to do exactly the work prescribed for it, but a tree, which requires to grow and develop itself on all sides, according to the tendency of the inward forces which make it a living thing. (1936: 117)

Mill always campaigned passionately for this cause but he limited it by insisting that it must be balanced against the danger of harming other people. One's own freedom, he said, is never a justification for damaging someone else. He was thus resigned to accepting a continual dialectic between safety and freedom, between public feeling and private wishes, between continuity and change, as being indeed endless, a basic, continuing part of the human condition.

The journey inwards, 2: Nietzsche

Nietzsche, however, was not resigned to this at all. He did, as we saw earlier, accept that the morality of custom had been a necessary training ground, an inevitable stage in the development of human culture. But he saw it as a stage that was due to pass, a condition that was becoming useless and even intolerable. Although he probably knew little about biology he eagerly accepted from Darwin the imagery of evolution: the idea that the human race was embarked on a one-way journey. And, like many of his contemporaries but quite unlike Darwin, he dramatized that journey in terms of his own moral perspective.

Just as social Darwinists like Herbert Spencer saw evolution as a progression towards the further development of capitalism, Nietzsche saw it as a progression towards more of the individualistic way of life that he favoured. Like Mill, he uses the image of a tree, but very differently. For him this tree is a means to an end, a tree with a destined function. As we have seen, in *The Genealogy of Morals* he tells us how "at the end of this tremendous process, where the tree at last brings forth fruit ... we discover that the ripest fruit is the sovereign individual".

The path to solitude

How is this individual to live? Certainly not just as he pleases. In *Beyond Good and Evil* Nietzsche imposes on him a remarkably stern discipline:

> One must test oneself to see if one is meant for independence and for command .... Never remain tied up with a person – not even the most beloved. Every person is a prison and a tight corner. Never remain tied up with a fatherland – not even when it most suffers and needs help (it is somewhat less difficult to untie one's heart for a victorious fatherland). Never remain tied up with compassion – not even compassion for a superior human being into whose rare torture and helplessness chance has given us an insight. Nor with a science. ... Nor with our own virtues which would sacrifice the whole of us to some one thing, to our hospitality, for example.... Never remain tied up with our own emancipation, that delicious bird-like distance and strangeness which soars ever higher ...
>
> One must know how to conserve oneself. That is the most rigorous test of independence ....

One must get rid of the bad taste of wishing to agree with many others. "Good" is no longer good in the mouth of my neighbour. And how could there be a "common good"?

(1974: 41–3)

Thus Nietzsche put the lessons in self-denial he had learnt in his Lutheran home to startling use: to isolate individual life from all the demands of those around it.

There is, however, surely something strange about this series of vetoes. If, as I suggested just now, we are seeing a dialectic between freedom and safety, we might ask: which of those ideals is being served here? The precept that one must *know how to conserve oneself* surely expresses caution rather than a call to adventure. And the detachment produced by avoiding ties seems much like that of people who are simply scared of human contact. In fact, the lifestyle that Nietzsche offers as a heroic policy of self-conquest is oddly negative; it can just as easily be seen as a nervous avoidance of all involvement with outsiders. This does indeed produce a kind of freedom and independence: freedom from claims, freedom from interference, freedom from commitment. But that only tells us once more what hopelessly thin, formal, negative ideals freedom and independence themselves are: how little sense they make on their own without the context of other aims to give them meaning.

Nietzsche, in fact, was being one-sided. And effective moral reformers almost necessarily are one-sided. The spur that drives their new insights is always horror of some special thing that is going on in their day, and we need to understand that horror if we want to use their message. Just as Hobbes was driven to call for individual survival by the futile brutalities that flowed from feudal thinking, so Nietzsche was driven to call for independent thought by the unrealistic slackness of his age: by its persistence in self-deceptions that misrepresented a sharply changing world.

Often his drastic demands for change centred on the charge that Christianity is anti-life:

> From the very beginning the Christian faith is a sacrifice, sacrifice of all freedom, all pride, all self-assurance of the mind; at the same time it is servitude, self-mockery and self-mutilation .... It is the Orient, the deep Orient, the Oriental slave, that took its revenge in this fashion against Rome and Rome's distinguished and frivolous tolerance. (1966: 46)

But his revulsions went far beyond objections to Christianity. What he hated most in the religion of his childhood was not, it seems, any peculiarly Christian points in it such as the threat of hellfire; it was the general falsity – the sentimental, self-protective refusal to see the dreadful facts of the world. And he thought this unrealism was every bit as strong in the secular creeds and ideals of the time. Indeed, he particularly hated utilitarianism.

On not being alone

All this is, of course, sound and powerful stuff. Good citizens and reformers are indeed often faulty people, sometimes moved by odious motives. Yet anyone used to seeing how changes actually get made in the world – or even how it keeps afloat at all – may well wonder whether a group of Nietzschean sovereign individuals would manage any better. Since they would all be well practised in avoiding the bad taste of wishing to agree with many others – quite free, not only from self-deception but from such weaknesses as compassion and desire for the common good – they would surely not find it easy to get together and do what was actually needed.

Nietzsche himself was, as is well known, a solitary. For most of his life his only contact with human society was made through thinking about it with extraordinary force and sending his thoughts out to it in his sharp writings. But he was really upset when he found that people would not save themselves by listening to his message. He did not simply lose interest in their fate. Until his health finally broke down he still tried desperately to get that message across to them. And a central part of it was that one must not cease to care: that there was no refuge to be found in Mephistophelian nihilism.

In short, Nietzsche took for granted the positive attitudes whose negative side he was so continually expressing. Moreover, he well knew that his writings were full of contradictions and he saw this, on the whole, as a virtue, in tune with the paradoxical nature of the world. It would have exasperated him to find himself treated – as some today do treat him – as an authority on morals, a guiding prophet offering simple, final solutions.

Conclusion
The wider perspective

In this book we have been looking at some of the thousand-and-one reasons why there can be no such simple solutions. The thing is that, as Darwin pointed out, a social animal that has imprudently let itself become aware of the clashes between its various motives is never going to find life straightforward. The work of harmonizing different aims must always go on. We do right to look for simplicity and to use it when we can find it. But we can never expect it – as seventeenth-century thinkers so often did – to be the final truth. We shall always have to do some of the work ourselves.

Darwin's enquiry seems to me really helpful here. Although it starts from an animal context it plainly does not reduce human qualities to those of other animals. It does justice to our special human difficulties and achievements. It centres on the recognition of conflict, on the clashes of motive that increasing self-knowledge must have gradually revealed to our ancestors, clashes that other animals too experience but briefly, since they live more or less in the moment. Our difficulty here – and our great blessing – is that we live in a much longer time perspective. Our longer memories are, as Darwin shrewdly pointed out, not just inert stores but active, interfering commentators, constantly reminding us of things that we would rather forget.

This means that other people are constantly present to us and must always be considered, so that mutual influence continually flows between us.

Thus, although each of us often needs solitude, in our essence we are not totally separate beings. At heart we are both separate and joined, and the interaction between these two conditions is what gives us both most of our joys and most of our problems. For our most precious occupations we need groups (think of drama, worship, families, football or choirs and orchestral music) and we identify with those groups. Yet there are also times, as Hobbes so rightly pointed out, when our own individual wishes rise up and demand absolute precedence. Balancing these claims is a central business for all human cultures.

Our life, in fact, is not a collection of solo performances but an immensely intricate large-scale dance in which solos take their place among figures performed by groups of the most varying sizes. I was struck by their variety myself when – having always been puzzled by accounts of people dancing in the streets – I found myself in Trafalgar Square in May 1945 celebrating the end of the war along with everybody else, and discovered how this dancing works. Concentric circles just form spontaneously and go round, making you feel, in a quite new way, at harmony with all the rest, however many they may be. And this feeling, which was new to me then, has remained with me ever since.

On the other side, too, we can sometimes feel strongly called to solitary action and this can sometimes turn out rightly. That happens particularly to young people, especially to teenagers, for whom indeed much of the recent post-Nietzschean individualist propaganda has been intended. They often need a solo, which, however, may end by bringing them into a new group. But, in anybody's life, these various phases have to alternate and they often do so unpredictably. They all go to form the richness of our experience. Within each of us, an often fractious dialogue between the need for solitude and sociability goes on continuously and makes an essential part of our life's riches.

During the past three centuries, however, we in the West have concentrated largely on the individualist side of this dialogue. For excellent political reasons we have kept on shouting for freedom, and have often managed to get it. We want many solos, but life, with its usual perversity, still remains as complicated as ever. Theorists such as Hobbes and Nietzsche who have simplified it on egoist lines have told us vital psychological truths, but we cannot accept them as despots. We need to put these matters in a wider context where the many sides of our nature are more realistically accepted.

On being grown-up

Most obviously this means that the emphasis on competition in recent political and economic thinking – the constant insistence on tournaments between individuals as central to human life – is a pernicious myth and the supposedly scientific story about evolution that has been used to back it is just a fantasy. Behind that story, however, lies a more general idea, crucial to the Enlightenment, about the centrality of independence in human life: an idea that, if we are adults, we ought always to act autonomously on our own – that it is childish to accept help or influence from anyone outside.

This voice in our culture tells us that, to achieve maturity, we must in the first place depersonalize nature: must not identify with it; must reject, as Christian thought had already done, the parental bonds that made pagans feel akin to the natural world and wholly dependent on it. It tells us, next, to stop depending socially either on other humans or on God, thus becoming completely free, self-creating, unmoved by any considerations from outside. As Sartre put it:

Man is nothing else but what he makes of himself ... Before that projection of the self nothing exists ... man will only attain existence when he is what he purposes to be. Not, however, what he may wish to be. For what we usually understand by wishing or willing is a conscious decision taken – more often than not – after we have made ourselves what we are ...

(1958: 28–9)

Or, in Nietzsche's words, "One must know how to conserve oneself. That is the most rigorous test of independence".

It is surely striking how this free self, in trying to conserve itself, seems to have shrunk until it has become only a rather mysterious fraction of the original. As Sartre saw, this precious fraction cannot include wishes, since wishes reach outwards and may have been produced by all sorts of outside causes, including physical ones such as hormones. I do not often quote myself, but something I wrote about this long ago in *The Ethical Primate* still seems to me right:

People who now see scientific determinism as threatening, but who still accept it, are forced to contract the moral self much more radically than Descartes did in order to preserve it from this threat. Like householders in a flood, they keep moving upstairs, gradually losing the use of their lower floors. More and more, what is free seems no longer to be the whole self but a distinct entity within it. Kant began this process and his followers are still continuing it .... The factors that menace that free self seem now not to be so much outside tyrannies ... but the remaining parts of its own nature. (1994: 114)

Thus, if freedom is necessary for maturity, a truly adult human would have to be one who has managed to shrink himself into this inner castle, no longer accepting any influences from the outside world.

This is surely a very odd notion of an adult state. We would, I think, normally suppose that being adult involves being able to act harmoniously *as a whole person*, being aware of one's various motives and able to bring them all together. And to do this sensibly involves receptiveness as well as activity. It calls on us to take in influences from the surrounding world eagerly enough to take part in it fully. That world, too, is a whole – a larger whole of which we are part; we cannot deal only with selected fragments of it. The dance of human life is only one figure in a larger dance that perhaps goes on for ever.

The trouble with the exclusive kind of humanism encouraged by seventeenth-century thought, which has developed during the Enlightenment, is that it is unrealistic. It has seen human intelligence not as organically linked to the material world, but as something separate, something higher and extraneous, an alien spiritual tribe, called on to exploit and colonize matter for its own ends. Rather remarkably, too, this inward-looking approach has survived the religious concept of spirit that was its source and has continued that tradition's disregard for the natural world – indeed, has intensified it – even in today's official climate of materialism.

In depersonalizing nature, humanism of this exclusive kind has surely replaced one set of myths by another that is no more realistic and far more destructive: an imaginative picture of the physical world as mere, lifeless, valueless matter, a dead world of objects without subjects, fit only to be appropriated by us. That is how we have come to do so much damage without even noticing it and have ended up understanding so little about our own continuity with what we were destroying. The kinds of individualism that we have considered in this book have played their part in distracting us from this damage, as well as in distorting our social and political life. We surely need to rethink them.

Bibliography

Atkins, P. W. 1987. *The Creation*. San Francisco, CA: W. H. Freeman.

Atkins, P. W. 1995. "The Limitless Power of Science". In *Nature's Imagination: The Frontiers of Scientific Vision*, John Cornwell (ed.), 122–33. Oxford: Oxford University Press.

Bunting, M. 2009. "In Control? Think Again: Our Ideas of Brain and Human Nature are Myths". *Guardian* (24 August): 27. www.guardian.co.uk/comment-isfree/2009/aug/23/brain-society-politics (accessed July 2010).

Butler, J. 1969. *Butler's Sermons and Dissertation on Virtue*. London: G. Bell & Sons.

Clay, J. 1996. *R. D. Laing: A Divided Self*. London: Hodder & Stoughton.

Conway Morris, S. 2003. *Life's Solutions: Inevitable Humans in a Lonely Universe*. Cambridge: Cambridge University Press.

Darwin, C. [1871] 1981. *The Descent of Man, and Selection in Relation to Sex*. Princeton, NJ: Princeton University Press.

Darwin, C. [1859] 1985. *The Origin of Species*. Harmondsworth: Penguin.

Darwin, C. 2002. *Autobiographies*. London: Penguin.

Davies, P. 2006. *The Goldilocks Enigma*. London: Penguin.

Dawkins, R. 1976. *The Selfish Gene*. London: Granada.

Dawkins, R. 1982. *The Extended Phenotype: The Gene as the Unit of Selection*. San Francisco, CA: W. H. Freeman.

Dawkins, R. 1986. *The Blind Watchmaker*. Harlow: Longman.

Dawkins, R. 1995. *River Out of Eden: A Darwinian view of Life*. London: Weidenfeld & Nicolson.

Dawkins, R. 2004. *A Devil's Chaplain*. London: Orion.

Dawkins, R. 2006. *The God Delusion*. London: Bantam.

Dennett, D. C. 1995. *Darwin's Dangerous Idea: Evolution and the Meanings of Life*. Harmondsworth: Penguin.

Desmond, A. & J. Moore 1991. *Darwin*. London: Michael Joseph.

Eagleton, T. 2009. *Trouble with Strangers: A Study of Ethics*. Chichester: Wiley-Blackwell.

Fodor, J. & M. Piatelli Palmarini 2010. *What Darwin Got Wrong*. London: Profile.

Goodwin, B. 1994. *How the Leopard Changed its Spots*. London: Phoenix.

Goodwin, B. 2007. *Nature's Due: Healing our Fragmented Culture*. Edinburgh: Floris.

Hobbes, T. [1651] 1931. *Leviathan*. London: Dent.

Hume, D. [1777] 1894. *An Enquiry concerning the Human Understanding, and an Enquiry concerning the Principles of Morals*. Oxford: Clarendon Press.

Hume, D. [1888] 1978. *A Treatise of Human Nature*. Oxford: Clarendon Press.

Humphrey, N. 1986. *The Inner Eye*. London: Faber.

Huxley, T. H. 1886. "Evidence as to Man's Place in Nature". In *Select Works of Thomas H. Huxley*. New York: John B. Alden.

Huxley, T. H. 1888. "The Struggle for Existence and Its Bearing upon Man". *Nineteenth Century* (February).

Huxley, T. H. 1893. *Evolution and Ethics*. The Romanes Lecture, pamphlet. London: Macmillan.

Kant I. [1785] 1997. *The Moral Law: Groundwork of the Metaphysic of Morals.*, H. J. Paton (trans.). London: Routledge.

Kauffman, S. A. 1993. *The Origins of Order, Self-Actualization and Selection in Evolution*. Oxford: Oxford University Press.

Kropotkin, P. [1902] 2006. *Mutual Aid: A Factor of Evolution*. New York: Dover.

Le Fanu, J. 2009. *Why Us? How Science Rediscovered the Mysteries of Ourselves*. London: Harper.

Midgley, M. 1994. *The Ethical Primate: Humans, Freedom and Immortality*. London: Routledge.

Mill, J. S. [1859] 1936. *Utilitarianism, Liberty, and Representative Government*. London: Dent.

Nietzsche, F. 1969. *On the Genealogy of Morals and Ecce Homo*, W. Kaufmann (trans.). London: Vintage.

Nietzsche, F. [1886] 1966. *Beyond Good and Evil*, M. Cowan (trans.). Chicago, IL: Henry Regnery.

Noble, D. 2006. *The Music of Life: Behind the Genome*. Oxford: Oxford University Press.

Peacocke, A. 1986. *God and the New Biology*. London: Dent.

Prigogine, I. & I. Stengers [1984] 1988. *Order Out of Chaos: Man's New Dialogue With Nature*. London: Collins.

Rose, S. 1997. *Lifelines: Biology, Freedom, Determinism*. Harmondsworth: Penguin.

Sartre, J.-P. 1958. *Existentialism and Humanism*, P. Mairet (trans.). London: Methuen.

Sloan Wilson, D. 2008. "Why Richard Dawkins is Wrong about Religion". In *The Edge of Reason: Science and Religion in Modern Society*, Alex Bentley (ed.), 119–36. London: Continuum.

Weinberg, S. 1977. *The First Three Minutes: A Modern View of the Origin of the Universe*. London: André Deutsch.

Williams, G. C. 1966. *Adaptation and Natural Selection: A Critique of Some Current Evolutionary Thought*. Princeton, NJ: Princeton University Press.

Wilson, E. O. 1978. *On Human Nature*. Cambridge, MA: Harvard University Press.

Wolpert, L. 1992. *The Unnatural Nature of Science*. London: Faber.

Index